THE LITERARY REVIEW

SUMMER 2009
VOL.52 / NO.4

AN INTERNATIONAL
JOURNAL OF
CONTEMPORARY
WRITING

All correspondence should be addressed to *The Literary Review*, USPS (587780), 285 Madison Avenue, Madison, NJ 07940 USA. Telephone: (973) 443-8564. Email: tlr@fdu.edu. Web: www.theliteraryreview.org. Periodical postage paid at Madison, NJ 07940 and at additional mailing offices. Subscription copies not received will be replaced without charge only if claimed within three months (six months outside U.S.) from original date of mailing. Postmaster, send address changes to *The Literary Review*, 285 Madison Avenue, Madison, NJ 07940.

Manuscripts are read September through May. We only consider online submissions of poetry, fiction and creative non-fiction. For more information go to www.theliteraryreview.org/submit.html

SUBSCRIPTIONS
One year: $18 domestic, $21 elsewhere; two year: $30 domestic, $36 elsewhere. Single issues: $7 domestic, $8 elsewhere.
Visa, MasterCard and American Express are accepted.
www.theliteraryreview.org

The Literary Review is a member of CLMP and CELJ. It is indexed in Humanities International Complete, Arts and Humanities Citation Index, MLA International Bibliography, Index of American Periodical Verse, Annual Index of Poetry in Periodicals, and the Literary Criticism Register. Microfilm is available from National Archive Publishing Company, P.O. Box 998, Ann Arbor, MI 48106. Reprints are available from the Institute for Scientific Information, 3501 Market Street, Philadelphia, PA 19104. CD-ROM versions are available from Ebsco Publishing, 83 Pine Street, P.O. Box 2250, Peabody, MA 01960-7250, and poetry can be accessed on CD-ROM through Poem Finder, available from Roth Publishing, Inc., 185 Great Neck Rd., Great Neck, NY 11021. The full text of *The Literary Review* is also available in the electronic versions of the Humanities Index from the H.W. Wilson Company, 950 University Avenue, Bronx, NY 10452. Selections from TLR are available online on the Infonautics Electric Library, www.bigchalk.com.

PRINTING BY WESTCAN PRINTING GROUP
78 HUTCHINGS STREET, WINNIPEG, MB R2X 3B1, CANADA

COPYRIGHT ©2009
FAIRLEIGH DICKINSON UNIVERSITY
A QUARTERLY PUBLICATION
PRINTED IN CANADA

ISBN: 978-0-9841607-0-9 0-9841607-0-1

PERMISSIONS
97: This story is reprinted from *The Most Beautiful Book in the World: Eight Novellas*, translated by Alison Anderson and published by Europa Editions, July 2009.

109: These poems are forthcoming from Farrar, Straus and Giroux.

151: These poems are from *Edward Hopper: Poems*, translated by Lawrence Venuti, forthcoming from Graywolf Press in October 2009.

MIKE SINCLAIR
FOURTH OF JULY #2,
INDEPENDENCE, MISSOURI

Mike Sinclair is an architectural and fine art photographer living in Kansas City, Missouri. His photographs are frequently published in the architectural press and elsewhere, including *The New York Times*, *Metropolis*, *Architectural Record*, and *Interior Design*. His work is in several public and private collections, including The Museum of Fine Arts, Houston, The Kemper Museum of Contemporary Art, Kansas City and the Nelson-Atkins Museum of Art, also in Kansas City.

The celebration in *Fourth of July #2, Independence, Missouri* took place on the lawn of the Truman Presidential Library in Independence, Missouri. The event, according to Sinclair, included speeches, introductions of prominent citizens, and a band concert featuring several numbers with a childrens choir. "I think," he says, "the Declaration of Independence was read aloud." The lawn was full of people—some picnicking, some just there for the evening fireworks display.

The haze in the picture is a combination of Missouri's humid summer weather, fireworks and smoke from the Civil War-era cannons that were fired while Tchaikovsky's *1812 Overture* played.

Sinclair will be in a group show at Jen Bekman Gallery in New York City in the fall of 2009.

Fourth of July #2, Independence, Missouri, by Mike Sinclair is available as a limited-edition print at 20x200.com, a fine art website that offers exhibition quality prints at ridiculously affordable prices, exclusively online.

For most of us, the last time we reflected at any length on the subject of Manifest Destiny was eleventh grade. And at that age in that context, the moral lines were mostly uncomplicated: "[*sputter sputter*] . . . EVIL Empire! . . . [*sputter*] Fascist pigs! And [*deep breath*] Ronald Reagan must . . . be . . . stopped!" The geopolitical borders had by then been drawn and the vainglorious motivations of great ships and flourishing empires were entirely yesterday's ineluctable stew. In fact, we chose this theme for our issue precisely because it is so essentially out of currency, elusive, and yet suggestive in a scurrying, spidery way. *Manifest Destiny*: by which we mean politics, ideology, the world, and heading off into the horizon to conquer. With literature. Bring on the rogue fiction, the expansionist poetry, Latin American bards, identity issues, culture bludgeons; bring on God, men, and guns.

And then the clarion call of bugles fades. "And then what, America?" —asks one of our poets, Bob Evans, here (quoting Milton Kessler)—"What if we have always had this, this more-than-we-had-ever-imagined?" For here we are, well into the twenty-first century. American imperialism creeps and staggers. It is no longer fierce, directed and ideological, but rather ambivalent, apologetic, deadly and political. It does not seem that we want *more* America (anymore); we simply want a more comfortable one. We "want" easier claims—on oil, technology, mobility, influence. We want greater access and less mystery. Less God, more gold.

As for glory, that most unquantifiable, third face of imperialism? Well, modern glory lies somewhere between Barack Obama and Michael Jackson. Exquisitely American phenomena, both; global in their reach, astonishing in their ascension— large bait for our collective dreams and desires. Self-invented, as Robert Polito points out in our interview with him; a determined combination of imagination and will, a conviction that there is some other, better way to inhabit this moment. How else would you define *literature*?

Minna Proctor
Madison, New Jersey

MANIFEST DESTINY

SUMMER 2009
VOL.52 / NO.4

Contents

CONTENTS

Kelly Cherry
Her Life to Come

She is seventeen, a freshwoman, as she calls herself. She is African-Italian-Cuban-Native American; the native part is Ojibway. She wears an earring in her eyebrow.

Like many seventeen-year-old girls, she plans to be a psychology major. Her own psyche fascinates her, fascinates her the more she becomes aware of it, and she feels that this gives her an understanding of psychology from which others could benefit.

If she doesn't become a psychologist, she might decide to be a Modern Dancer. Both the mind and the body interest her, especially her mind and her body.

She loves the university, its buildings with crenellated tops, the huge live oaks, some with Spanish moss, some with ferns clinging to their limbs, and the football weekends when the Seminoles play at home. In her dormitory room in Tallahassee, with its very cool collector-item posters of Stokely Carmichael and Lucille Ball, she records her thoughts and feelings in the journal that was her going-away present when her parents left her here at the start of the school year. She tries on different handwritings like jeans, wondering which suits her best. Some of her friends keep diaries on Internet web sites but she prefers to make her entries in bed, just before she turns out the light.

At the moment, she is experimenting with different ways of writing her name. *Ramona Maria Prairie Moonlight Ysglesias*, she writes, with her pink-ink felt pen, on the inside cover. Today is a holiday, Martin Luther King, Jr. Day; spring-semester classes don't start until tomorrow. Her roommate has gone off to swim in somebody's pool. "You should come with us," she said, as she gathered her swimsuit and sunblock, but Ramona preferred the cool of their air-conditioned room. It is hot, a hot day in January. All over town, the palmettos, the poinsettias in big pots look as if they'd burn your fingertips if you touched them.

In the next moment Ramona's telephone is going to ring. She doesn't know this, but it will, and she will pick up the receiver. It will be her mother, who will tell her she has to come home because Ramona's father has killed himself. He has hanged himself in the bathroom.

Ramona loves college; she loves how her mind is filling with ideas and facts. Up to the brim! Every day she wakes up eager to learn something else. She can't wait to start on courses in her major and just last night was reading the text for Advanced Deviant Psychology, although majors don't get to that class until senior year. She has not yet answered the telephone, but when she hears the word "bathroom" she will, even while feeling guilty about it, wonder why her father chose the bathroom and if he really did choose it or if his death was a sexual accident like the ones in the chapter titled "Auto-eroticism," but as soon as the shock fades and she begins to cry, she'll forget her first shameful thought and remember that her father was forced into early retirement last year, that he is—*was*—melancholy by nature (he said it was the Ojibway in him), and that her mother and father had not been getting along. They had vicious, screaming arguments, each calling the other worse names than they had been called. Ramona will find herself throwing clothes into her backpack and sobbing at the same time, grabbing her sunglasses as she flees the room, the pack over her shoulder, heading for the bus station. She will never see her dorm room or her roommate again.

At twenty-three Ramona will work behind the counter in a copy shop. She wears high catch-me heels and eyeliner and that earring in her eyebrow. She has smooth skin, a light bisque shade, and the irises of her eyes are almost as dark as the pupils, which makes them look as large as almonds. She can be pensive. Sometimes her friends say to one another, "Ramona has a secret," but they never ask her what it is.

When her friends ask about her ethnic heritage, she explains that she is African, Italian, Cuban, and Indian. She says it is the Ojibway that gives her trouble. "My father's father came from Minnesota to work in an orange grove," she tells them, "but he missed the Thousand Lakes, the state bird, the snow drifting silently between hemlock and spruce. Ask me what is the state bird of Minnesota."

"What is the state bird of Minnesota?" they ask.

"The mosquito," she answers.

They groan and roll their eyes, but she continues: "He was homesick, so he put up a tepee in the backyard. He left his wife and children, including my father, in the house and moved into the tepee. Night after night his wife waited for him to come in. When she could no longer keep her eyes open, and only then, she turned off the light and went to sleep.

"My grandfather lay in his tepee, looking at the sky through the hole in the top. If he squinted, he said, he could make the moonlight look like prairie moonlight along the Iowa border. So my father named me Prairie Moonlight."

"But your name is Ramona," her friends protested. "Ramona Maria."

"That's true," she said. "And it is also Prairie Moonlight."

She will marry within the year. A budding lawyer comes into the shop, wanting to make a lot of copies that no one in his office will see, and she shows him how to use the machine with the collator and automatic stapler. He is lean, with a sharp-edged, sexy face, the kind of face that can cut a woman's heart to shreds, but he wants her. He wants her every which way and everywhere. They will marry at his folks' place in Miami. At the wedding, her mother cries. Her mother is wearing a beige suit that shows off her young-looking skin, and navy blue shoes. Ramona Maria puts an arm around her mother's shoulders and coaxes a smile onto her face. Reggae and salsa blast into the summer night. A film of sweat covers bride and groom, like Saran Wrap. The groom kisses his bride on the top rim of an ear. She flashes her eyes at him, rolls her hips when she walks in front of him. The party goes on until daybreak, but she and her groom leave at one in the morning, the stars still bright above the Atlantic. The wind is rising and the hairs on her arms stiffen in response.

Dave slogs away in a firm where most of the cases are divorce cases. Sometimes there are personal injury lawsuits to file. That's about it. Ramona Maria will feel sorry for her husband and try hard to bring some fun into their life together but she does not get pregnant in spite of their efforts. She will visit her doctor, let him do an endometrial biopsy and start her on fertility drugs. She will make Dave leave work to come to the doctor's office with her. They will circle dates on the calendar tacked to the inside of the door of the bedroom closet. When they have sex, it will be half-heartedly, because they are afraid to risk more disappointment. Finally, Ramona Maria will discover that she is pregnant, but before she can call her mother to tell her the news, she cramps and bleeds. Dave will find her lying in bed when he comes home—at six-thirty in the evening.

He will stretch out beside her, except that he is in his suit and on top of the sheet while she is under it and in her nightgown. He will listen while she tells him what has happened. He will sit up then, stack the pillows behind him, and pull her head onto his lap. He will whisper comforting words to her as if she were the lost baby and not the would-be mother. Strands of her long hair, which has a satiny Native American feel to it along with a tendency toward wayward Italian waves, stick to her face, which is wet with tears, and he will pry the stray strands away one by one. She will look up at him and see the underside of his clinched chin, the bones in their wedge of skin.

The next time she miscarries she does not tell him. She does not want to upset him.

They live in a ranch house in a subdivision where all the houses are ranch houses. Blinds and curtains are drawn against the relentless sunshine. Water bugs struggle out of the bathtub drain. Outdoors, slender lizards drape themselves over rocks as if they were at a Roman banquet. Small striped scorpions keep an eye on things from pockets of darkness between porch steps, under the house, beneath bushes. At midday, the neighborhood is silent and yet the sky seems like an invisible wire twanging a high note and she can't get it out of her head. She counts her blessings. He doesn't beat her, doesn't lord it over her. He still makes love to her, but he stays late at the office.

Eventually they will talk it over, and he will move out. "Where will you go?" she'll ask, and be surprised when he says, "I've been seeing somebody. We've decided that I'll move in with her." For a moment, she will not be able to breathe.

Two weeks after he leaves, she will discover that she is pregnant. She is twenty-nine when she becomes a mother, and she will have twins, because of the fertility drugs. Dave will come to the hospital when she goes into labor, but after the twins, a boy and a girl, are born, he will go home to his girlfriend, also a lawyer.

Her mother will help with the kids, at least until Ramona Maria can get on her feet and on a schedule. At thirty-five she will work at a juice stand at Disney World in Orlando. The twins are in school. She applied for a job as Minnie Mouse but it went to a college kid looking for summer work.

She will go back to college herself. She can take a class now and then, she will realize, and sooner or later it will add up. Instead of studying psychology, she will enroll in Information Technology. She will be an IT girl.

In her class on information systems, she will meet a compactly built former high-school basketball coach with skin as black as a moonless, starless night. He is thirty-eight and has a thirteen-year-old daughter from a former marriage. Her name is Athaliah, from the Bible. Perhaps Ike and Athaliah's mother had not actually read

When the downstairs neighbor complains, Ike says, in his irresistible honey voice, "Hey, man, come up and meet my family," and the neighbor will come up, wondering why the hell he let himself be dragged up like this, and the kids'll start to dance around him.

the Bible, or they would have found another name. The biblical Athaliah was the daughter of Ahab and Jezebel and she arranged for the murder of all the male children in the royal family. On weekends Ramona, Ike, the non-biblical Athaliah, and Running Deer (Ramona calls him Running Deer although to the outside world he is Joey) and Violet dance to hip-hop in the living room of her apartment, and when the downstairs neighbor complains Ike says, in his irresistible, honey voice, "Hey, man, come up and meet my family," and the neighbor will come up, wondering why the hell he let himself be dragged up like this, and the kids'll start to dance around him, their arms in hip-hop motion, their legs like an assembly line, their bodies making quick jive spins as if they were turning on a dime. And the neighbor will be unable to help himself and will dance with them.

She will think she has found her future. She will bring her man into her bed and into herself and in class on Monday night they will both blush, relieved to know no one can see it.

She *has* found her future, at least for now. She marries him at the courthouse, a justice of the peace presiding, Athaliah, Joey and Violet all standing next to them. Athaliah's mother comes to the apartment to pick up her daughter and says to Ike, in front of Ramona Maria, "I hope you make this work. She's too nice for you to treat her the way you treated me." Running Deer and Violet have frosting smeared all over their faces, and Violet is wearing the plastic butterfly from the cake in her hair.

When does it go wrong? She will never know for sure. They are so busy—the twins to be looked after and ferried around, her job, his job (he is working in sales at a chain computer store), night classes, cooking, cleaning. "Pay attention," her mother says in an email, but everything else needs attention, too. Ike's daughter falls in with a bad crowd, tries Ecstasy and coke and starts mainlining oxycontin, runs away from her mother and asks Ramona if she can live with them, but then she doesn't come home to Ike and Ramona, either. Ike has trouble in his classes, starts to fail, makes wisecracks about how his wife is smarter than he is but not so smart that she didn't have the sense not to marry him. She tries to be patient but slips up and shouts, "You're right! I don't know what I was thinking!" and the twins start to cry, which they some-how manage to do with their whole bodies, and Ike yanks his leather jacket off the back of the couch and slaps his hand over the pack of cigarettes on the dinette table and slams the door on the way out. Ramona swallows a handful of aspirin and wish-es she had a tepee she could move into, a place where she could lie down and look up at the moon and stars.

For a time after her second divorce, she will refuse to go out with men. "I'm busy," she will tell them; "my children and my classes take up all my time." She gets her children to read to her while she's cooking dinner. She takes them to the park on Sundays. On some days she can get her studying done while she's at work. At last, at forty-four she will receive her Bachelor of Science. The twins, now fifteen years old, are in the audi-torium when her name is called and she walks across the stage to shake hands and be handed her diploma. They cheer her from their seats. "Way to go, Mom!" they cry, and strangers, moved by the kids' pride and enthusiasm, take up the shout and now the whole room is yelling congratulations: "Way to go, Mom!"

She will examine her face in the mirror, see the fine lines branching beside her eyes, the almost imperceptible sag of her jaw, the slight lengthening of her nose, and think the day may have come when she should have the earring removed from her eyebrow, she's too old and it is—how can this be? but it is—old-fashioned. Body piercing belongs to the past, but she remembers how Running Deer would tug on it when he was an infant, drawn by the bright silver, the shiny coolness. She remembers his tiny fist, his fat little fingers patting her face, the way he cooed and babbled and that she had to keep blinking for fear he'd poke her in the eye, and she leaves the earring alone. Even though Running Deer has long since announced that he will answer only to "Joey."

When the twins are ready to go off to college, Ramona will breathe more easily. Her face will relax, the netted eyes will soften, she will let herself gain a few pounds and the result will be a calmer, less severe Ramona, and middle-aged men will look at her and wish their wives were as easy-going, as willing to let their bottoms sway and the tops of their breasts show over the circle necks of their tee-shirts. They will wish their wives had not hacked off their hair saying that only young women can wear long hair. They will wish their wives wore earrings in their eyebrows.

Ramona will meet one of these men three years later in the software company she joined as a manager of business services. He will see her one day when he passes the open door to her office, and he will walk into the office and introduce himself to her. He's about five-ten, gray at the temples, the hairline receding, he wears a wedding band and a class ring, and his face is pockmarked. He is rich, too rich, she assumes, to take her seriously. She will sleep with him without expectations and be surprised when, some months later, he tells her he loves her. He wants to leave his wife for her. "Oh, no," she says, "that would be awful." "Not for me," he says, "awful for you?" "Awful for your wife." "She'll adapt," he says, and she doesn't doubt it—hasn't she herself adapted plenty? But it's never been easy! "It's hard," she'll say, "it's hard to change your way of life." "It's for the best," he answers, and adds that they will honeymoon on a yacht in the Keys. Indeed, they will be married on the yacht. The setting sun will turn the blue water purple. Dolphins will leap out of the water and dive in again. Pelicans will fly in battery lines, their wings turning the water beneath black. The next day, docked in a cove, at breakfast, Ramona and Gerhardt will drink fresh orange juice and nibble on croissants, and Ramona will already know that she has made a mistake. She has married three times, and probably she was never meant to be married even once. She tilts the brim of her sunhat farther over her face. The water is splashing gently against the hull. Gerhardt has gotten up and is behind her, bending over her. He kisses the back of her neck. She bursts into tears.

He kneels beside her, asks her what's wrong.

She can't tell him she has just realized that he bores her to death. He bores her to tears! She can't tell him she hates that he left his wife for her. That she hates herself for it, and she hates him for it. She especially can't tell him that somehow, annoyingly, bafflingly, incredibly, she hates his now former wife for causing all this trouble. "I don't know," she will say.

She will have to do better than that. She will say that she misses her kids, even that she has trouble understanding how it is that they are now at the University in Tallahassee. She tells him about the day when she was seventeen and her mother called to tell her that her father was dead. She tells him that the bus home took her through Panacea and Sopchoppy. She will tell him that *Creature from the Black Lagoon* was filmed in Wakulla County, but he won't have seen it.

After this conversation, she will begin to like Gerhardt better. She will decide that she is fortunate to have found a man as sympathetic and caring as he is. Ramona no longer has to work but she keeps working because she enjoys it. They have a house-keeper, and Ramona enjoys that, too, enjoys how they live a very good life, with cars that are not a struggle to get in and out of, with weekend dinners at the country club where she can look in Gerhardt's direction and pretend to be listening but be seeing, through the huge, fanatically clean window behind him, the rose bushes, the bougainvillea, and what must be the greenest golf course in America, and doing all of this in nice clothes. When Athaliah turns up on the doorstep of their white brick Colonial house, her nose running and her arms covered in tracks, Ramona will be confused. She will want to remind Athaliah that she is not her mother, that she, Ramona, Ramona Maria Prairie Moonlight Ysglesias-Parks-Freeman-Schmidt, is no longer married to her father, that, in fact, Athaliah is no kin to her at all, but looking at her, the messy hair, the chewed, peeling lips, she will take the child from Athaliah's arms and fold him into her own while telling Athaliah to come inside and put her suitcase down.

"Thank you," Athaliah says, meekly, and when she does, Ramona sees that she has needle marks between her fingers, too.

"Who is this?" Gerhardt says, back from nine holes on a Sunday afternoon.

"This is Athaliah," Ramona says. "Athaliah, this is my husband, Gerhardt Schmidt."

Athaliah extends her hand. "Pleased to meet you," she says.

Gerhardt shakes Athaliah's hand and looks at Ramona to let her know that he has seen the tracks on Athaliah's arms.

"And this is—?" Ramona says, ending in a question mark.

"Coltrane," Athaliah says. "Cole for short."

"Cole," Ramona says.

"Hello, Cole," Gerhardt says. Cole pushes his face into Ramona's neck.

Gerhardt disappears into his home office.

Ramona looks hard at Athaliah, but the girl, skinny, wearing a sundress, and with dark circles under her eyes, refuses to meet her eyes.

Athaliah says, "Is it all right if we stay here? Because I don't know where else we can go." Before Ramona can ask about Ike or Athaliah's mother, Athaliah says, "I'll do whatever you want. I'll get clean. I'll get a job. Please, just help us."

Because Athaliah says *us* instead of *me*, Ramona takes Cole into the kitchen with her and tells Aberdeen that there will be two more people living in the house from now on. She will explain to Gerhardt after they get into bed for the night, after Athaliah and her son are asleep and Gerhardt has done his half-hour on the bicycle in front of the late news and while she is moisturizing her hands with an almond-smelling cream. "I don't want you to do this," Gerhardt will say, once again surprising her. She had thought he would go along with anything she wanted. "We shouldn't have to do this at this point in our lives. She can stay here until she's back on her feet, but then it's out they go."

"I'm sorry you feel that way." Ramona does not think that Athaliah will get back on her feet, though naturally she hopes she will.

"What are you saying? Ramona, you work. You have volunteer activities. You have a son and a daughter in college. Don't tell me you want to start all over."

"No," she says. "I don't want to." She will have noticed that he has neglected to mention his own three children, all adults, one in Brownsville, one in New York, and one in Chicago.

"Then that settles it."

"I guess so," she will say. "I guess it does."

But what exactly has been settled? she'll ask herself. She has said that to appease him, but nothing has been settled yet. She thinks that what Gerhardt wants is not to be bothered.

The world will have changed quite a bit since she was seventeen, and in ways she never could have forecast, but a child in need will still be a child in need. She will tell her mother about Athaliah and Cole and that Gerhardt doesn't want to be bothered. "Then don't bother him, but you can't send the child away. He needs a mother." Her mother is living in a small condo with a beaded curtain dividing the kitchen area from the dining area and plants in pots on the small balcony.

Ramona will find Ike's current email address and let him know that Athaliah is with her. She will insist that Ike forward the information to Athaliah's mother. But neither Ike nor Athaliah's mother has ever known what to do about Athaliah, and they are willing to let Ramona handle the situation. *It is not a situation*, she thinks, *it is a life*, but if she said this, they would only feel chastised, and they already hate themselves, so she says nothing. She doesn't think it helps anybody much for people to hate themselves and so many people do. She and Aberdeen look after Cole while Athaliah is in detox, and then a halfway house, but then Athaliah starts using again and disappears. Ramona Maria looks everywhere, she goes to the Missing Persons Bureau, she hires a detective. Now Ike and Athaliah's mother can blame her for their daughter's disappearance, but they still don't want to claim Cole. Joey and Violet bring presents for Cole whenever they come home, for Christmas, Thanksgiving, sometimes for their mother's birthday. Violet uses an Afro comb on his hair and pulls too hard and Joey chases the tears away by singing to him. For some reason, he sings "Oklahoma."

Somewhere along the way, Gerhardt grows used to the idea of Cole. He begins to treat Cole like a son, taking him to the zoo to see the alligators, telling him bedtime stories. Ramona never reminds Gerhardt of what he said when Cole first came to the house. Cole goes to school and grows up.

Ramona moves her mother into assisted living, then into a nursing home. She will visit as often as she can and hold her mother's hand. Her mother is wearing the comfortable Ojibway moccasins Ramona ordered online and gave to her. In her nineties, her mother has fallen silent, like snow drifting between hemlock and spruce. They will sit together peacefully for a half hour.

She will brush her mother's hair. She will clip the spiky hairs that grow from her chin and that her mother can no longer see. She will straighten her mother's room. She will water the cyclamen in the flowerpot on the windowsill.

Cole is a grown man, a graduate student in geology at the University of Washington in Seattle, when Ramona learns that her mother has died. It is not unexpected but neither is it expected: there had been no indication that her mother was failing physically. She had been at the home for so long that the nurses feel they have lost a friend. The nursing home will offer to help Ramona make arrangements. Ramona will drive to Tampa the next day.

In the sideview mirror she will see herself as an old lady, almost seventy, her hair gone completely gray, her eyes sunk deeper into the sockets although the dark spark of them is still there. She is wearing a white blouse open at the throat and sees that her neck has gotten creepy, the skin tissue loose. A pair of reading glasses dangles from a chain around her neck. Her hands on the steering wheel have liver spots. With her bisque skin, the spots don't yell Look at me!, but they are there. She thinks she looks pretty good for an old lady, but, she reminds herself, that doesn't change the fact that she *is* an old lady. She pulls off the highway and into a rest stop and goes into the Ladies, where she removes the earring from her eyebrow, starts to put it in her purse, and then drops it into the trash container.

At the nursing home she talks with the resident doctor and the building manager, and then she visits the funeral director who has an agreement with the home and the bank where her mother kept her Last Will and Testament in a safe deposit box. The funeral, which will be small but respectful, is scheduled for Monday, to give her mother's friends time to make plans to attend. Ramona carries empty cartons, provided by the home, to her mother's room and starts sorting items for the Salvation Army, Joey and Violet and Cole, and to throw away. Her mother distributed most of her belongings before she moved in.

Going through her mother's things, Ramona will eventually come across the journal she kept in her first semester of college. Her father had given her the notebook as he and her mother were leaving her on campus for the first time. He'd cleared his throat, that fastidious, elegant man, and brought it out from behind his back. "You'll have so many things to talk about," he said, "and you won't want to talk about them with us. So this is for you. . . ." She will not have realized that it had wound up with her mother. She will turn to the first page and on the inside cover see her own name, her given name, in pink ink. Was she really that young once, young enough to keep a diary in pink ink? Startled, she will lift the reading glasses and prop them on her nose, the chain drooping from the tailpiece over each ear. She will marvel at her name as it pitches forward across the page, or curls up like yoga, in rounded letters, or marches with the excellent posture of toy soldiers, or falls backward, like someone not ready to be where her feet already are. She will close her eyes for a moment. Except that she is old, she might be back in her dormitory room in Tallahassee on an unseasonably hot day in January, dreaming of her future, when the phone at her elbow rings.

But today, Martin Luther King Jr., Day, she is seventeen, and the phone at her elbow is ringing.

Clea Roberts
I Have a List of Things

I cast no shadow. I follow the cart's lopsided squeak.
I follow the girl with the lettuce-colored hair
and shoes thick as phonebooks
past the perfect tubes of toothpaste,

past the rubber balls in wire cages,
inhale the off-gassing,
fluorescent air around us.

A boy plays the game with the robot arm
plucks zebra, giraffe, a panda for the baby.

Today he is eight and generous with the world
and loves babies but would hurt them,
and the next day forget, and hurt them again.

Shopping at Wal-Mart is that easy.
I glide between the things that people need and want
separate the lovable from the unlovable—

our souls jangling like quarters,
as full and as empty as plastic bags
rolling in the wind.

We Loved to Eat at Burger King

Let's not forget when we were young
our paper crowns nodding,
never having entered
the pastures of our mortalities
or figuring the hoof to square yard ratio.

We laughed, our thoughts and kisses
light as Styrofoam.

Death was a small, under-populated town
where cats and hamsters eventually traveled,
our grief contained in the manageable handkerchief
bundles swinging behind them.

Meat was an erotic vegetable, its marbled currents
swimming on the kitchen counter, the elastic weight
slapped in the frying pan while our mothers tutted
about our fathers, their indiscretions and commutes.

I remember those days as the first days.
Somewhere in the backyard, my sister stuck pussy willows up her nose
and I fell in love with the kitchen wallpaper,
its pale yellow roses so open, all they could promise was an end.

Technology

All those November
black-out babies,
some kind of proof that technology
interferes with us.

How we discover ourselves in the dark
as animals, thickened with urges,
urges that take us in hand to demonstrate
the twitching limb,
the woman splitting herself open.

Maybe it's phone calls
during your lunch hour.
Maybe it's knowing too much
about Britney Spears.

Maybe like sea turtles
we can't determine
between the patio light
and the authentic light of the moon—
so we don't know which way
to move in our bodies.

But if everything relents
and you have your first thoughts
about the freezer contents and then
of resetting the alarm clock,
what then do you think of
sitting in the dark
with one candle burning
between us, and the hum and tick
of the refrigerator gone.

Jennifer Louise Percy
Training Ground

Mornings, we slept in military tents. Evenings, we sat on faded, pink-striped lawn chairs and watched the sun die. We were surrounded by lava fields and black dunes, plants I didn't know existed, the hum of a military chopper. Everywhere palm trees curved and rotted. I was working in Volcanoes National Park, Hawaii, getting paid forty dollars a week to tag and monitor endangered sea turtles along the Big Island's southern coast.

To prepare for the field our boss gave us each a walkie-talkie, a waterproof field notebook, a flashlight, a burn kit, an emergency cell phone. We had a truck check, a pack check, a boot check. He gave us all camo pants and army hats and we wore heavy packs and we were dropped off at the bottom of a road that fell two thousand feet from the jungle to the coast. We formed a line and hiked along the black sand.

Our boss, Will Cody, ran the program out of a house in the jungle with funds from the National Park Service. He usually wore short-shorts and ripped shirts and his socks were always pulled up past his calves. The house had two rooms, five desks, a Mac from the late '80s. The walls were covered in topographic maps, anatomical sketches of turtles and their shells. There was a dead turtle by the computer, trapped in a bottle of formaldehyde, and every time I came in the office it faced a different direction. We were in the field for two weeks at a time, in groups of three or four, sometimes in pairs. On our days off, we stayed at the Kilauea Military Camp—just a mile walk from Will's office. I lived with two girls in a house outside the military camp. The Kilauea Military Camp is a sixty-acre plot of grass and trailer homes and bad restaurants, full of American flags and picnics and men sitting on benches. It used to be a training ground for the National Guard but now it's a resort, a vacation destination for soldiers. For a while, on my days off, I just wandered around the camp eating macadamia nuts or going to the Volcano Museum. Sometimes I took walks around the rim of a nearby crater, watching the tourists crawl around its yellow insides. At night, I went to the Lava Lounge with its electric signs and wilting flowers and little tubs of fake lava made from curled plastic and red bulbs, and I would find the retired military officers drinking and wearing camo and slapping each other on the back, talking about AK-47's and Vietnam and how sometimes they wished they were back there, in the dark, wrapped in creeper vines, sinking into the mud. It's where the boys who wanted to be soldiers came to drink; the boys who were soldiers—the boys who might have just returned from Iraq or Afghanistan—who might be shipping off in a C-17 tomorrow, in a month, a year.

I would go to the Lava Lounge and find them drinking Miller High Life with their heads down. I'd walk by them, between them, going to the bathroom or to get a drink, and though sometimes I would put a hand on one of their shoulders to excuse myself, getting close enough to smell something like wet wood, they remained where they stood, absorbed by their own voices. Dreams still clung to them—I could see it in the way they shaved every morning, how they crossed their legs like folds of paper.

The Lava Lounge is where I'd find my boss dancing alone, his long, greasy hair let loose in the fluorescent light. The first time I saw him at the Lava Lounge he was sitting in a cloud of smoke with a group of soldiers, a woman with tattooed eyebrows, and a park ranger named Kelly. He wore a military uniform and had his hair tied back in a neon scrunchie.

So what was it like? What was it like when you got shot in the face? Will asked one of the soldiers wearing a gold earring. The soldier smiled, and the scar, looking like a wad of chewed gum, pulsed like it was alive. He told everyone it was like dying but not in that way, another way, like something that you didn't know was there had died inside you, and you miss it even though you aren't really sure what it was or if it was there at all.

Tattooed eyebrows said bull-shit. She took a drag, went to piss.

A soldier at the table with crow-colored hair sat quietly and drank his beer, looking into his bottle before each sip. He asked what I was doing, and then we drank together and three songs played, and then I fell in love and we decided to climb Mauna Loa. That night I imagined our bodies together on the top of the volcano, my feet facing the ocean, his facing the sky.

His name was Luke and he was twenty-three-years old and a soldier at the Pohakuloa Training Area just outside of Volcanoes National Park.

There are 45,000 military personnel in Hawaii. Most of the military bases used during WWII have been converted into training grounds. The Pohakuloa Training Area (PTA) is the largest in Hawaii and it's used year-round for aircraft and ground-troop training by all branches of the US military. They use rifles, mortars and howitzers in what the local paper terms "the closest approximation to combat short of war." Near the PTA, on the slopes of Mauna Kea, is the Bradshaw Army Airfield Facility, which supports the 25th Infantry Division and its associate units: Wheeler and Schofield Barracks, the Hawaiian Army National Guard Hilo, and the 45th Support Group.

They died before they even went to war. Some of them dying in ways no one knew you could die. Maybe that was the whole point.

While I was on the beach running sunscreen up my leg, people died around me. I read the articles in the *Hawaiian Tribune*: Soldier killed, three injured when a hand grenade exploded during a night training accident at Schofield. A soldier with the 65th Battalion killed and four injured when a mistake was made rigging two Bangalore torpedoes at the PTA. Six soldiers killed and eleven injured when two Black Hawk helicopters collided during a night training exercise. Etc.

They died before they even went to war. Some of them dying in ways no one knew you could die. Maybe that was the whole point.

When I was in the field, sitting in my pink-striped lawn chair or crouched in the bushes counting turtle eggs, I thought about the soldier. I'd often imagine that I was with him on the training ground, that my cot was a real military cot, and that at night I would lift my headlamp not to illuminate a turtle but a face, pale in the dark. I wondered if he was also awake night after night in the darkness, not knowing why he was here.

When I was a kid my family lived in Kaneohe Bay, Oahu, and our neighbor was a retired military officer. He was a muscular old man but for a heavy, swollen gut. Sometimes I would see him standing in his lawn following the glint of distant planes landing at the Kaneohe Bay Marine Air Station. One summer he had a garage sale and he sold me a knife, a box of war movies and a wristband that said ROCK. I wore the wristband around my bicep and started telling people my name was ROCK. Sometimes at night, from my bedroom window, I would spy on him. If I was lucky I would see him moving from each yolk-colored room to the other, lifting things, kicking the air, dancing as if in combat. I watched him as I would watch an adult film I did not understand.

To save the turtles we had to kill mongooses: packs of them that lived in the dunes. The first time I killed a mongoose I was at a beach called Apua Point. The beach was all black sand and black water. A volcano in the distance seeped and glowed red at night. I was with Will and two girls: Cam, short and butch, and Jess, just the opposite. Cam said she once saw a mongoose eating a baby turtle: it was red and soft like a piece of cherry pie.

We set up twenty cages on the dune and baited them with tuna fish and cat food. At night I heard the cages falling one by one, a metallic clank followed by quiet screams. In the morning, when the sky was pink and the ocean looked solid and hard we put on our boots and climbed the rocky dunes. Will was wearing one of his desert storm hats and an unshaved beard that went all the way down his neck.

He found the first mongoose and called us all over to look at it. He stood over the animal with his leg bent, his back straight.

He showed me how to kill it properly. I needed to put on the special leather gloves and keep a finger on the metal release switch as I lifted the cage into a white garbage bag. He showed me which way to turn the orange knob on the carbon dioxide tank, where to place the long black tube that fed the gas into the bag.

I turned on the tank and the mongoose reached a hand against the bag as if to remind me of its form. The bag grew and I wanted to sympathize with the mongoose, imagining my lungs filling with the stale gas, but Will paced around me, checked his watch, and when I looked into the bag five minutes later the mongoose was curled and taken by gravity.

I killed ten mongooses before I saw my first turtle. It was as big as me and completely black. Colonies of other creatures lived in its shell. When I found the turtle I waited until it was halfway up the beach and then got down on my stomach and crawled over the black sand, following it into the bushes where it nested. I watched by the light of my headlamp as she buried hundreds of plum-sized eggs beneath the earth. When she finished, taking care to cover each egg with sand, I wrapped her small head in a towel and held her jaw closed as I pushed myself onto her wet back. She dragged me towards the ocean while I punctured each flipper, leaving her with a metal tracking number.

Sometimes people would appear in the middle of the night and find us on lawn chairs watching the ocean. I imagined that for some time they waited and observed us from the shadows. The way the metal legs of our chairs sank heavily into the sand, how through the faded pink stripes of the lawn chair they might have been able to discern the silhouette of our torsos, the bend of our legs. They must have watched how we spoke, how we moved, what we ate and drank, how we dealt with boredom. Eventually they emerged and walked onto the sand and said something casual.

Once a group of soldiers came to our camp in the morning when we were still sleeping. I woke up and they were sitting among us. They wanted some of our water and we gave it to them. As a way of saying thank you, one of the soldiers climbed a palm tree, cut down a coconut with a machete and carried it to us. He rolled up his sleeves. He made lunging motions. Then he smashed the coconut with a machete, and when it opened, white and clean like a bloodless wound, he poured rum inside each half and passed it around the camp.

One soldier named Edwin didn't really say anything when he came to our camp at night. Sometimes we would wake up and he would be sleeping among us, tangled in a hammock between two palms like an insect caught in a gossamer of thread. He was tall, corpse-thin and wore delicate glasses that he was always cleaning. He said he was just checking on things, monitoring the beaches. Every once in a while we would be hiking, sweating among the black rocks and bleak sky, feeling our bones dry and our muscles eat themselves, and he would lap us, walk right by us whistling a tune, and then disappear back into the heat from which he came.

Everything became monotonous. The flies that covered our bodies, the ants in the water jugs. Usually I just tried not to pass out from the heat. I started to forget about the turtles and why I was there and I remember one time I killed a mongoose and I was surprised at the thrill I felt looking inside the cage. I buried it in the ground and put a rock on top of it.

I didn't hear from the soldier for weeks and then he called me on the emergency cell phone. He said the Mauna Loa plans were still on. We met at the Lava Lounge on an empty night when the sky was clear and the air was even a little bit cold. At the bar, insects swarmed the ceiling. They left their oily casings piled in the corners, in the ashtrays, the curved rims of plastic lamps.

Will was with the military guys on the red leather couches whispering things to the Lava Lounge girls. They were dark-skinned girls: Filipino, Indonesian, African, Chinese. I watched their mouths open, their heads fall back. There was a young Japanese girl wearing a muumuu made of purple and white fabric, her lashes matted from humidity and laughter. I watched my boss watch her take a shot, thinking about her delicate brown neck. Her body defined and damp. Later that night, I found the white petals of her lei pressed in seat cushions, floating on the wet bathroom floor.

The only time I met Luke outside the Lava Lounge was when we went swimming at a pool that was about two hundred degrees and tucked into a swampy area right next to the ocean. It steamed and made everyone swimming inside look ghostly and old. The pool was surrounded by mango trees that left their yellow fruit to stain and rot the cement. I hoped that when we jumped in we would disappear into the steam and then into the sky so he wouldn't have to go to war but we didn't because when we stepped into the water we just looked pale and human.

When he arrived, the bartender sat atop her bamboo stool and stared at us, eating small pieces of pineapple. I could see the yellow pulp in her teeth. He ordered bourbon. I flattened a napkin across my lap and ordered the same. But we didn't talk about Mauna Loa because last night his friend was shot by a machine gun. He's fine, he told me. It got him in the arm.

We held each other in the red light of the Lava Lounge and I pressed my nose into his shoulder, smelling the fabric of his uniform. For a time, I let him touch me, let his hand work up my thigh. I knew we wouldn't climb Mauna Loa. He knew he might not be back, and he told me this, and I realized that it didn't matter because he was already somewhere else.

When the eggs hatched in late summer, Will led us to a nest marked by white coral. He showed us a turtle, just born, wilted and brown like a dish rag, half-buried in the sand. It took hours to push itself out. Hundreds followed. We counted them, we took notes. They were covered in mucus, eyes shut. Some died on the way to the ocean, some died when they dived into the water breaking their necks in the waves. A mongoose came and took the smallest ones away. I got up to help the stranded turtles but Will told me that wasn't protocol so I just sat on the beach and watched them die and began to understand why Will was here, why he always wore a uniform and said things like OVER and OUT, and made us sleep on the black beaches along the Kilauea lava flow for nights and days waiting for the turtles. I thought about the uniform heavy on his back, how it must have seeped into his skin, molded his face, his eyes, the way he spoke. I thought about the soldiers and how the uniform gives them a sense of moment, of being. How it let them look someone in the eye with blood all over their face and smile and say *it will be okay.*

Jerald Walker
Two Boys

The two boys were in the backseat screaming for their mother, who was behind them in the parking lot, dying of a bullet wound to the thigh. The fact that Steve had shot her in a leg lets me hope he wasn't trying to kill her, but his lawyers would not make that argument during his trial. They would simply portray him as a victim, a person who should be pitied and prayed for, as if he, like the two boys, had also been strapped in a booster seat, speeding from a mall with a killer.

He let them out just before pulling onto the street. They ran back to their mother, not comprehending her non-responsiveness because they were only five and six. They would not be called to testify.

Steve's girlfriend Katrina would. While he performed the jacking, she'd sat in an adjacent car, also stolen, watching with horror as a long prison sentence played out before her. Her lawyers would ask the jury for pity, too. They'd explain how Steve, without telling her his intentions, had driven Katrina to the mall, parked, told her to get in the driver's seat, and then approached a blue Intrepid, pointed a gun at the driver, and ordered her to get out. The twenty-eight-year-old victim whirled and lunged for her sons. Steve fired through the window. When Katrina is asked why she didn't flee, she would testify that she was too afraid, citing Steve's history of physical and mental abuse. Just the night before, he'd beaten her and then locked her in their bedroom while he went to find them more dope. She saw no choice, she'd tell the jury, than to follow him, just as he'd commanded.

They headed east on 79th Street, weaving recklessly through the two-lane traffic. When I read this part of the court transcript I remembered Steve's love of drag racing, how he'd challenge any drivers who were teenagers like us. The challenge taken, we'd hit speeds of sixty or more where the limit was only thirty, plowing through stop signs and red lights, seeking, it seems in hindsight, evidence that we were mortal. We didn't find it then, but the proof is surely upon us now, as my hair has thinned and grayed, and Steve sits on death row.

. . . seeking evidence that we were mortal. We didn't find it then, but the proof is surely upon us now, as my hair has thinned and grayed, and Steve sits on death row.

The sentence was rendered in 2007, six years after the crime was committed, six years after I completed my PhD. My twin brother called me with the news because I no longer live in Chicago where we were raised. My wife and our children live in a small town in Massachusetts, the kind of place that doesn't produce junkies who shoot mothers. Chicago's South Side, on the other hand, is a factory for such people, rolling them out like so many assembly-line toys, each seemingly no different from the other. That apparent lack of distinction was why, during the trial, court-appointed lawyers offered the same tired excuses: a life of poverty, an abusive father, a neglectful mother, the tormenting want of love and attention. And that is also why the jury turned a deaf ear on Steve's defense, and on Katrina's, too.

I did not know Katrina. It is fair to say, by the time Steve committed this murder—his *second*—I did not know him. The last time I'd seen him was in 1984. My girlfriend Pam and I had just scored some coke and stopped at a liquor store when Steve, as he always seemed to do, swaggered from the shadows. A woman clung to his arm. I invited them back to my apartment to get high. Steve and I had lost touch for a few years because he was in and out of jail, but while it was good to see him again, it was also uncomfortable; I had already begun to doubt my commitment to the thug life, whereas he seemed to be embracing it tighter, wedding himself to a brazen lawlessness that frightened me. Proof of this came late in the night, long after we'd all turned in. Pam and I were in our bed, while Steve and his friend were in the living room on the couch, both asleep, I figured, as I passed them on my way to the bathroom. But when I returned a moment later, Steve was gone. And then I heard Pam scream. I ran into my room just as he scrambled off the bed, his boxers bunched at his heels. It was the kind of foolhearted act for which men have lost their lives, and yet at that moment I felt, for some reason, that *my* life was the one in danger. My voice trembling less from outrage than fear, I told him to leave. He went to the couch and woke his female companion, yelling at her as though the whole thing had been her idea. As she dressed, she cast me a quick glance; perhaps remembering the hopelessness in her eyes is why I cannot help but feel sympathy for Katrina, even though I did not know her, and even though her version of events may not be true.

"I didn't know he had a gun," she testified, insisting that she thought they were at the mall only to shoplift. I believe that. I believe her, too, when she said she deliberately caused an accident in order to attract police. A young man whose pregnant wife was in the passenger seat was driving the car she rear-ended. The man got out to inspect the damage, and then he went to confront Katrina. Steve pulled beside them and told her to drive away. She did. Steve did, too. The man ran back to his car and gave chase. When he caught up to Katrina and began yelling profanities through the window, Steve shot at him twice. The man took off, heading west. Steve and Katrina, still in their separate cars, went east.

Steve wanted to find a chop-shop. Katrina said she knew where one was on the West Side. They made several stops

along the way—a liquor store, a gas station, Katrina's mother's house, her sister's, closer and closer to a place that did not exist; Katrina had made the whole thing up, simply trying to buy more time. When it seemed to be running out, she caused another crash, this time hitting two parked cars, the impact with the second being so violent that her car flipped and threw her to the curb. Witnesses descended from all directions. One of them had called for an ambulance before telling her help was on the way. Steve, pretending to be just another concerned witness, pushed through the crowd and said he'd help her now. He asked for and received directions to the nearest hospital, and then he picked up Katrina and put her in the Intrepid. As they drove away, he pressed the gun to her temple. It's difficult for me to imagine that, by then, a part of her didn't want him to pull the trigger. When the police captured them a short while later, I suspect it was one of the happiest moments of her life.

Steve now sits among the condemned, awaiting execution, and I sit in my study, looking at his photo. It is posted on the website of the Pontiac Correctional Center. For many years I've toyed with the idea of going to see him. I've reviewed the visitation rules and regulations, and I even priced tickets from Boston to Chicago. I have imagined us sitting across from each other, separated by three inches of Plexiglas and both of us holding phones. I know we'd spend the hour recollecting the better times of our youth, how we'd made out with girls in his brother's immobile Mustang, or the dance moves we rehearsed before going to house parties. We'd mention the first times we got high, and then our forays into petty crimes, the botched ones making us shake our heads and smile. "Remember that time," one of us might say, "we tried to steal a whole goddamn *case* of beer?" When we'd erupt in laugher, the other inmates and visitors would look our way, wondering what could be so funny, and Steve and I would know that, behind this lighthearted veneer, nothing actually was. He was going to be executed, and I was not, even though we were both assembly-line toys, manufactured with parts that weren't intended to last. Mine had—he'd hate me for that. But I'd hate him, too. Because for the entire visit, I'd be thinking about *my* two boys, ages six and eight, and imagining them in a world, for no good reason, without a mother.

R.A. Allen
The Emerald Coast

There was no breeze. The Gulf's blue-green surface was flat, and a haze—the waning vestige of a morning fog—hung above it. Listless waves mopped the tide line like a careless janitor. Waitron lit a cigarette and half-leaned half-sat on the wooden railing that enclosed the al fresco deck of Joe's Crab Trap. It was the mid-afternoon lull: bartenders prepping fruit garnishes for happy hour, busboys sweeping up sandy French fries, and the wait staff trudging through the personally unprofitable side-work demanded by management in order to save money by not actually hiring someone to clean mirrors, dust woodwork, polish stainless steel, and whatnot.

Because of the haze, the glare was diffuse and everywhere and it burned into Waitron's retinae even in the shade of the deck's canopy. The haze muffled the beach noises: children squealing, the thump of a volleyball, snatches of music, the shrieks of gulls. He scanned the long white shore from east to west for as far as he could see. How many females could he discern between the vanishing points of his sight? Three hundred? More than five hundred? Certainly less than there were in August.

The need within him was rising, building like steam, his need for sex-plus. Sex-plus was a fulfillment that, he knew, average men never dreamed of; but it was his ultimate gratification. It came at a price, though, and the price was the need itself—the wanting—which was like hunger and thirst and a drug craving rolled into one. It was time to mark this territory and move on. He was first out in the shift rotation tonight and would be packed up and headed for Colorado in a few days, disappearing back into the floating world of the seasonal waiter. The time was right, like planets aligning in his favor. He would have to find the right one. He would try tonight.

"Robert?"

It would be Holcomb, the day-shift manager; the only one who addressed him by his real name. Hands on hips, Holcomb was standing just inside the doorway. He said, "You think you might dust the paddle fans anytime soon?"

Because he was tall, this was one of Waitron's side-work duties. He dead-eyed Holcomb for a beat or two. "When I finish this," he said, ashing his cigarette on the plank floor.

Holcomb went back inside.

There was nothing else Holcomb could say and they both knew it—the season was ending. Waitron turned his attentions back to the beach. How many between the ages of twelve and twenty-four? How many with the correct hair? The right body?

Now a hammering noise broke his reverie—a man replacing shingles atop the main building of the restaurant. Waitron watched him with detachment. The roofer was one of those construction worker types that, a few seasons ago, were everywhere in Destin. Scruffy hair and beard, shirtless and tanned impossibly dark, one of the numberless rabble drawn from the rural areas of the Southeast by the building boom now fizzling out along the Emerald Coast of the Florida Panhandle. He was just under medium-sized, monkey-built, a creature of sinew and vein. He wore a tool belt over cutoff jeans and a pair of filthy tennis shoes. To Waitron, he was a perfect specimen of his class: a cracker, a variety of Georgia/northern-Florida white trash whose life revolved around semi-skilled labor, cheap beer, and trailer park squabbles. It must be 120 degrees up there, Waitron mused—how does he stand it?

As if he could feel someone staring, the roofer stopped work and eased into a squatting position against the low slope of the roof, forearms resting on his knees, hammer dangling from one hand. He stared back at Waitron. The roofer had a crude tattoo— an eye—on his left triceps. A warning floated up from Waitron's memory. The roofer continued to stare at him with pale eyes set in a hawkish face. Waitron turned away.

Oakley paced the balcony, grinding on the mood he was in. "They call us trailer trash," he said. "And because the world has tarred us with this appellation, we are condemned to a brutish existence."

"I reckon what we're called is an accident of our births," Sparrow responded mildly. "I don't *feel* like trash." He'd been pounding nails since five AM in the broiling heat. Now freshly showered and in clean clothing, all he wanted was to relax with this beer while the sun set on the beautiful Gulf below. "You read some Hobbes when you were up in Fountain?"

"Yeah, I read *Leviathan*. I read that copy of *The Peloponnesian War* you sent. I read a lot. Ain't nothing changed: you do your forty-cent-an-hour job, you do your reps at the weight pile, you go to chow when they call you and you sleep when it's lights out. There's still lotsa time left over to advance your education."

"You didn't go Mao-Marxist on me did you?" Sparrow joked.

"Nah. I'm just saying . . ."

Oakley had been out for three weeks. His doomed fascination with a jewelry store up in Dothan had bought him a stretch of two years and ten months.

Sparrow and Oakley had been best friends since grade school in a nameless, sun-struck tract of Section Eight housing on the outskirts of Mary Esther, Florida—itself a strip mall of a town that owed its existence to neighboring Eglin Air Force Base. They had shared the highs as well as the misery, looking out for each other in stir and out.

They were on the balcony of Oakley's second-floor crash in the old Spindrift Motel, a fifties-era relic, now condemned—pilings washed out by a June hurricane had destabilized the western wing. By this time next year, the pastel high-rise depicted on the billboard out front would take its place. Oakley was living there on the sly through the beneficence of Two-Eleven, the Spindrift's one-time handyman, now caretaker-cum-watchman pro tem and old jailing buddy to them both. It was no big deal to Two-Eleven, as he figured to be let go when the developer sent the dozers in—which might be any day now.

With two hundred feet of sand-covered extension cord, Oakley was stealing enough electricity from the absentee owners of the condo next door to power a refrigerator, a fifteen gallon hot water heater, and a couple of lamps. There was no A/C, but it was late September, so the heat was tolerable for sleeping—just. Money for the necessities came in from day trips as a deckhand on the charter boats out of East Pass, baiting hooks for tourists, cleaning their catches, swabbing the decks and gunnels, lugging ice—the flunky work of a nautical factotum. But Oakley, not one to take direction in the first place and chaffing at the dictatorial manner of the charter captains, was gaining a reputation as a malcontent on the marina. His other source of income, he'd told Sparrow, was "odd jobs."

They watched a young couple stroll out to the water's edge and settle onto a blanket. For Sparrow, the girl added a carload of black chips to the quality of the beachscape. She was a stunner, a corn-silk blonde not older than twenty. In defiance of a municipal ordinance laid down by the local guardians of social order, she was wearing a thong—coral in hue, a mere afterthought in terms of beachwear. Sparrow shivered. "You get laid since you got out?"

"Went and saw Amber a couple of times while that sheriff's deputy she moved in with was on duty, but she's turning into a candidate for *Girls Gone Wild*."

Sparrow remembered the hot-and-haughty Amber. He emitted a dry laugh.

Oakley studied the thong girl for a moment and then looked away, as if the sight of her caused him pain. "I got money on my mind, bro. I lack funding. A man can't be who he really is without money. Which brings up my next point: I need to find Davy Redstone."

"Davy Redstone the fence?"

"Yeah. He owes me three dimes from that pawnshop B-and-E that I pulled before I went in. I heard he's hanging out at a bar north of the 331 Bridge, a slop chute called the Owl's Head. I need you to go with me. I need you to watch my back."

"That was four years ago. Redstone's gonna balk on you."

"I will stress to him that a debt is a debt. He gives me any shit, I'll have to tune him up."

Sparrow nodded. He did not doubt that the prospects for *violencia* were distinct, if not imminent. Along with the alpha-dog precepts of your seasoned convict, Oakley had the muscle and the martial portfolio to back up a volatile nature. Problem was: Redstone traveled with an entourage. If it came to a dustup, they would be bucking the law of superior numbers.

"He'll have his homies cheek by jowl," Sparrow said.

"I got no choice."

"I'm there for you, bro."

Watch my back was the undeniable—the unquestionable—call for support between them. And Sparrow's response was gold-standard true, true at the risk of incarceration, true past the point of injury, true *unto death*. It was his duty to a bond forged out of old hard times.

Along with the alpha-dog precepts of a seasoned convict, Oakley had the muscle and the martial portfolio to back up his volatile nature.

Duty. At one time, Sparrow would have greeted violent confrontation in service of this bond with gritty cheer. But he had turned thirty-three in March. Somewhere, Sparrow had read that thirty-three is an introspective watershed for even the thickest of men: they come to the sit-up-in-bed realization that times are flying. Like the tolling of a giant bell, it had been no different for him. He had been into some kind of criminality since the age of twelve—all of it larcenous, some of it violent, most of it with Oakley. But during his latest left-handed endeavor, Oakley had been behind bars. It was in collusion with an Atlanta-based counterfeiter—a former penitentiary colleague—that Sparrow spent two months passing bogus twenties in the Caribbean. The Feds were waiting for him at the gate at Miami International. On a half dozen surveillance videos, he starred as the prosecution's witness against himself.

The government confiscated everything they could find; what they couldn't find, his lawyer wound up with. He'd bargained for thirty months and maxed it out at the Federal Correctional Institution in Marianna. It wasn't that he couldn't do the time; it was just that, in the joint, the judicial system is eating the front end off of your future.

Right after his release, he'd met, fallen in love, and moved in with Marlene, a clerical for a bail bondsman in Fort Walton. She had a four-year-old daughter who adored him for no reason whatsoever. So he had come to a conclusion: He didn't care if he had to be a roofer or a ditch digger or a dishwasher for the rest of his life, he wasn't going to do any more time. He had a duty to Marlene. And for little Jonquil, he was going to be the father he'd never known. Would Oakley understand his duty to them? Sparrow didn't think so. Right now, he wished he were at home with them, watching TV. But Marlene was up in Waycross visiting her mama, which was why he now found himself here with Oakley. He hoped they wouldn't find Redstone.

"When do you want to go?" Sparrow said.

"Now."

"My truck is on empty."

"We'll take my car."

"When did you get a car?"

"The other day. It's parked over in the Hampton lot. Keeping it around here might draw attention to my living arrangements. Grab the rest of them beers. Let's go."

Sparrow gave the beach a wistful last look. The wind was picking up.

The Hampton Inn was a two-block walk east on Scenic 98—the original beach-view part of Highway 98—and two blocks north. There was no view of the Gulf from this Hampton, and it attracted the folks that couldn't afford one—kids, mostly, or blue-collar families who scrimped to give their children a few days at the beach. From the rooftops, Sparrow would see them: mom, dad, and their youngsters, shuffling along in single file—serious as mourners—on the white gravel shoulders of the beach-access streets, wearing their sandals and bathing suits, loaded down with towels, coolers, floats, umbrellas, and other beach crap.

Oakley's ride was a late model Taurus. Sparrow got in and took its measure. "You boosted a rental," he said, checking the column.

"Yeah. But the plates are fresh."

"Goddamn."

Oakley was grinning like a dog eating cheese. "Don't worry, bro. I'll drive safe."

"Hi, folks, I'll be your waitron for your dining experience tonight," he said—his standard icebreaker that generally evoked a smile from patrons. "Would you like to start with a cocktail?"

The party was comprised of two fortyish couples and a teen-aged girl—a daughter, he supposed. The adults wanted cocktails. While they decided, Waitron eyed the girl. Her hair was all wrong—too long, too light.

Leaving with their drink order, he noticed a lone girl at the bar. She was correct: petite, shoulder-length brunette hair, early twenties. Her face was okay—a poor man's Drew Barrymore. The glasses were an added attraction. By coming in here with that sluttish haircut, she was begging for sex-plus.

This was his last table. If the girl at the bar stayed until his checkout was over, it would be another sign.

She reminded him of number four, decomposing now for some two years in a hole fifty yards into a wooded area off of Highway 7, a few miles outside of Norwalk, Connecticut. Like the others, he had her GPS coordinates committed to memory: bargaining chips that would keep him off death row in case they caught him.

The sun went down. His table decided against dessert, but, to his annoyance, one of the women wanted coffee. He checked on the girl at the bar. She'd just ordered another margarita. His luck was holding.

After Waitron finished with his checkout, he marked time at the waiter's station, rolling silverware in paper napkins and watching the girl. Finally she finished her drink and paid, leaving, not by the door to the lot that bordered Scenic 98, but down the steps to the beach. Perfect. Waitron felt his nostrils flare; felt his lungs fill to the bursting point. He counted to ten and exited by the front door. He jogged through the parking lot to his car, where he grabbed the sack that contained the things he needed and then walked around the outside of the building to the beach. Her white shorts made her easy to follow as she walked eastward, barefoot in the surf-dampened sand.

Oakley had the pedal flat on the floor on their way back across Choctawhatchee Bay, speedometer bumping 110. The Taurus was bucking like a jackhammer because, having whacked a parked truck on their gravel-slurring escape from the Owl's Head, the front end was out of alignment.

"Feels like we're coming apart," said Sparrow, gripping the armrest.

"We gotta get off this bridge," Oakley said. "If they called the five-o's, we could get bottled up."

Sparrow thought his prayers had been answered when they walked into the Owl's Head to find that the fence was not there. They'd hung around for a while at the bar, casually pumping an evasive bartender about Redstone, and otherwise minding their own business.

Evening dissolved into night. The Owl's Head was a dive and it possessed that seething atmosphere that all dives have, but things remained peaceful until a girl who was all teased-up hair and quick movements came up and wanted to know about Oakley's shamrock tattoo like it was some kind of message aimed at her from outer space.

Turns out: there was a narrow-minded boyfriend.

Oakley knocks boyfriend's eye out of its socket with a backhanded blow from a two-pound beer mug.

Boyfriend's friends materialize.

They fought a rearguard skirmish to the door, Sparrow swinging a barstool; Oakley brandishing the Spyderco folding knife that he kept clipped inside the waistband of his jeans.

The Taurus gained the causeway at the end of the 331 Bridge. A second later, they had to swerve to miss an SUV pulling out of a tourist trap called 3-Thirty-A.

Sparrow sucked his teeth. "Slow it down, willya."

Oakley dropped it down a notch or two. He said, "Ninety-eight is only a mile away. We get there, we'll be in good shape."

Sparrow wasn't so sure. Their remaining headlight was beaming off at a crazy angle, and they were trailing smoke like a crop duster. "We're gonna have to ditch this vehicle PDQ," he said.

"Wonder where that fucking Redstone was," said Oakley.

When they got to Highway 98, they headed west into sparse traffic. Just east of Sandestin they passed a Florida Highway Patrol cruiser on the opposite side of the highway. The patrolie's head snapped in their direction as he went by. Sparrow turned around and saw the cruiser's roof lights come alive. "We got an audience," he said.

Oakley made a U-turn at the next opening in the median just as the cop was doing the mirror-image same 1500 feet behind them. With his shirttail, Sparrow started wiping down the armrest and everything else he could remember touching.

"Damn," said Oakley. He slammed to a stop in the emergency lane. "Good-bye, Taurus."

They sprinted down a weedy embankment and vaulted a three-strand barbwire fence. Beyond the fence, they were quickly swallowed by the dense ground cover of a pine savannah. Branches whipping their faces, wiregrass snagging their feet, they crashed through. The highway, pulsing with blue light and echoing the squawk of a radio, faded behind. Saw palmetto spines stabbed through their jeans. Overhead, the slash pines cast bottlebrush silhouettes against a pumpkin moon.

Simultaneously, they tripped over a fallen log.

"What place is this?" Oakley puffed.

"Topsail Hill Park. It's a nature preserve," said Sparrow. "If we can get through it, we'll come out on deserted beach."

"How do you know?"

"I re-roofed the park office and the pavilions in April. I read their brochures at lunchtime. The wind is blowing in off the Gulf. All's we gotta do is keep the breeze in our faces."

The sandy soil turned mucky, and suddenly they were chest high in cattails, and next, in water up to their waists. They backed out, lily pads clinging to them like greasy bandages.

"What now?" Oakley wanted to know.

"We stumbled into Morris Lake. If work our way to the left, we'll run into a tidal marsh that drains it into the Gulf. We can follow it to the beach."

Twenty minutes later, they found Morris Lake's outfall; they felt their way along its edge, aided by lightning flashes from a storm percolating out over the Gulf.

"Yow! Shit!" Oakley yelped. "Something bit my leg."

"You see what was it?"

"Too dark. Them brochures mention snakes?"

"Yeah, got cottonmouth and rattlers, but a bunch of non-poisonous ones, too."

They could hear the surf now. A few minutes later, the scrub broke onto a twenty-five foot sand dune crested by sea oats. The outfall creek, brimming with tannin-blackened water, cut through the dune and became an estuary flowing through the beach and into the Gulf. They clambered up the dune. Cloud-to-cloud lightning and intermittent moonlight delivered the blessed sight of the beach below them. A constant, storm-driven sea breeze drove the waves onto the shore with the intensity of a cymbal roll; salt spray stung their faces. Oakley tried to roll up the leg of his jeans to inspect his wound, but his calf was too swollen. "Pretty sure it was a snake," he said. "My leg's gettin' stiff on me."

Sparrow said, "We gotta walk two miles of this beach to Sandestin. We get there, we'll get you into the emergency room at Sacred Heart."

Mushing through the soft sand atop the dune, it quickly became apparent that their best time would be made on the more compact surface of the beach. They slid down the face of the dune. They could taste the storm's ozonic breath. An in-rushing cloudbank canceled the moonlight.

They walked along the base of the dunes, pushing west toward the lights of Sandestin's high-rise condos. The wind sheared their faces like a belt sander, and, more rapidly now, lightning fluxed cloud-to-cloud and into the water at the horizon.

"I thought you said this beach was deserted," Oakley said, pointing toward the water's edge.

The next lightning flash revealed two figures in copulation—a man was taking a woman from behind. They were facing the sea. The lightning bleached their skin a cadaverous white.

"Haw," said Oakley. "It's the doggy-style remake of Burt Lancaster and Deborah whatsherface on the beach in *From Here to Eternity.*"

It went dark.

Came another long flicker.

"Something ain't right about this frame," Sparrow said.

"True that. Let us file for discovery."

They strode closer, their approach masked by the roar of the elements. The man had something twisted around the woman's neck—a rope or belt—and her arms flopped like those of a rag doll with each thrust. In a voice loud enough to be heard above the combers, Oakley said, "Well, well, if it ain't Chester the Mo-lester. In the slam, we got a cure for you rape-o motherfuckers: it's called sticking my pecker up your comic-opera rectum."

He was skinny and basketball tall and he leapt away from the girl like he'd stepped on a third rail. The girl collapsed face forward onto the sand. Sparrow noted that her back was cut to shreds.

The guy got his pants up and lunged toward something metallic—a bowie knife—that was sticking out of the sand.

"He's got a banger!" Sparrow yelled as the man swept the foot-long blade in a wide arc toward Oakley's face.

Like an exercise-yard assassination, they split to either side of him. Sparrow heard Oakley's Spyderco snap into locked position. The man feinted at Oakley a second time. Oakley tripped backwards into the sand; the man moved in on him, bowie knife poised to plunge. Sparrow snagged the man's elbow, clutching it just long enough to keep him from stabbing Oakley. The man rounded on Sparrow. Sparrow threw a fistful of sand in his face.

The man made a noise in his throat and reeled backwards, clawing at his eyes. Oakley was on his feet again. "Eat this, Chester," he said as he jabbed his blade into the guy's midsection and then ducked beneath the reflexive chop of the big knife. Taking advantage of his opponent's blindness, Oakley cut the man repeatedly with his own blade, slashing and pinking, a quick gash across the forearm, one that missed the groin to strike the man's upper thigh. Sparrow thrust-kicked at the man's knees, trying to take him off of his feet, but either missed or landed glancing blows.

Oakley's hit count mounted, but three-inch wounds to the torso of a man whose bloodstream is blazing with adrenaline are hardly felt, much less immediately fatal.

At the water's edge, they spun in a death dance played out in total darkness punctuated by the blinding strobe of the lightning. Finally, Oakley managed to sink the full length of his pocketknife's blade into the man's lower ribcage; the man gasped. Sparrow tripped him, but as he fell, his blind thrashing with the heavy-bladed hunting knife caught Oakley across the belly as he was rushing in. While the man was trying to get back up, Sparrow kicked him in the temple and then again at the base of his ear. The man's grip on his knife went slack. Sparrow wrenched it free from his grasp and, with his left forearm pinning the man's throat, plunged the blade in and up through the man's solar plexus. Blood geysered into Sparrow's face. The man convulsed orgasmically for five seconds and lapsed into shock. Twenty seconds later he was dead.

Oakley was lying on his back in the sand, the front of his shirt soaked with blood. Sparrow bent over him and said, "Hey, bro. You okay?"

Oakley's eyeballs were rolled up. "Between the river and the steep came . . . serpents," he mumbled.

Sparrow shook him. "What? What's that mean?" He tried blowing into Oakley's mouth, but Oakley remained incoherent. Sparrow went over to the naked girl and rolled her over. She was limper than a boned capon. He splashed seawater on her; she made a noise. She was alive—for now.

Far down the beach, he saw headlights coming toward him. Sparrow rubbed a handful of sand on the handle of the bowie knife sticking out of the man's chest. To wash out his tracks, he sprinted along the edge of the surf, back to the natural ditch that Morris Lake's outfall made in the beach, and waded up its dark waters until he was safely back among the pines.

Soon, the airspace above shoreline lit up with beams and flashes of light—red, yellow, blue, and blue-white. Sparrow heard the helicopter and then saw the probe and sweep of its searchlight, the angry finger of society's god. He crawled beneath a gallberry bush. It was starting to rain.

Sparrow spent Friday night in the preserve. The rainfall varied from blinding sheets to drizzle. During the drizzle, he worked his way west through the brush until his terror of stepping upon an alligator or a snake in the darkness finally made him stay put in a thicket of swamp sweetbells.

Saturday blossomed hot, and the sun reached across ninety-three million miles to beat him like a child. He fell asleep from exhaustion in the middling shade of a scrub oak, but, an hour later, awoke in a panic of hot needle stings that were everywhere. Ants! He was covered in them. They were biting his face; they were in the crotch of his jeans; their mandibles clung to the dried blood of his many cuts and scratches. He hurdled through the shrubs to the blackwater depths of Morris Lake and—gators and snakes be damned!—plunged in. For the rest of the day, he holed up in a fetterbush in the lee of a dune. No one came in after him.

Well after dark on Saturday, he emerged from the bush—famished, dehydrated, mud-slaked, bug-bitten, and now ravaged by poison ivy—to make his way up ten miles of beach to Destin. If he came across late-night beach strollers or kids out crabbing, he would hide in the surf up to his chin and wait until they had passed.

Around three o'clock Sunday morning, Sparrow reached his truck.

The Sunday evening TV news said Oakley was in the ICU in a coma and that some waiter identified as Robert something-or-other was dead (good riddance) and that a girl—apparently a victim of a violent assault—was in critical-but-stable condition and was expected to recover but couldn't remember anything about what had happened. There was no mention of a fourth party, but Sparrow knew that the cops don't release the full story.

They'd come for him or they wouldn't. Oakley would live or he would die. Sparrow could accept that Life was bigger and more agile than he was.

Around nine o'clock, Sparrow heard a car door slam and then footsteps on the iron steps that lead up from the driveway slab to the kitchen door of their mobile home. Marlene and little Jonquil were back from Waycross. Sparrow, slathered in Neosporin and hydrocortisone cream, was sprawled on the couch in a pair of boxers.

Marlene's dropped her suitcase when she saw him. "John," she cried, "what happened to you?"

"Nothing."

Hesitantly, she asked, "Are you okay?"

"Yeah."

Jonquil came in behind Marlene and clutched her mother's leg. "Is Daddy John hurt, Mama?"

"No, darling he's okay. Go put your things in your room. Mama will fix you some supper when she gets unpacked," Marlene told her daughter, turning the child toward the rear of the trailer. "You want another beer, John?"

"Yeah."

"And you're sure about 'nothing' happening to you?"

"Yeah, I'm sure."

"Okay, then," she said as she headed for the kitchen.

Sparrow looked at the TV but it wasn't much in the front of his mind. Marlene wouldn't ask about it again. This was the way it was among their kind.

Miciah Bay Gault
City of Lonely Women

The town I grew up in is famous for two things. One is granite, which supposedly made my great-great-grandparents rich. The old quarries are still there, empty and echoing, the jutting ridges of which we climbed as children. Like magic, one generation finds itself rich on the pinkish blue stone the earth burps up. Like magic, the next generation can't sell the stuff to save its life. Poof! The quarry is deserted. The bosses leave town. Empty houses, empty storefronts. The jewelry store turns pawnshop. The barbershop is a brothel. The history of Woodfern is a magic act in which everything disappears. The show ends, the magician goes home with his doves. But the people of Woodfern stay late into the night, scouring the stage for all they've lost. Jobs, self-respect, children's legacies. They at least want their money back! This show stinks, they decide. Give them back their seventy-five cents! This is the legacy they pass down to their children and their children's children: the treasure of the thwarted, that heirloom resentment.

Into this I was born. A town of people mad at God and no relief for it, although they tried various methods over the years. Drinking only got them in trouble with their wives. Fighting took too much energy. They tried starving their own dogs and that gave them some satisfaction. They killed every deer, squirrel, moose, bear, fox, coyote, turkey, grouse, and duck within the legal limit, but a forestful of dead beasts couldn't make up for what they'd had and what they'd lost.

Other boys my age picked up their parents' discontent like hand-me-down boots, but I was different. While other boys could experience every shade of anger known to man, every black and blue hue, I knew something about love. I knew that love was not a single stroke of feeling, not the solitary stab of an arrow or a thunderbolt, but a rich and wild condition that varied in its visitations the way storms did. Love could be turbulent like wind or as gentle as rain.

The way I loved my mother was of the gentle variety. In its day-to-day form it was a dull throb of gratitude, but it could be sharpened suddenly, breathlessly, by her faintly dusty, wintry smell as she took her coat off in the hall; tightened by a rare eruption of her teenage beauty rising from beneath the pale and faded mother I knew.

The love I felt for my father was stiff but comfortable comparatively. He was a vegetable farmer, with a wheat-colored beard and huge cracked boots he wore year-round. It was our tradition to spend Youth Day at his camp by the lake, waking up at four in the brittle dark to wait for deer. The sharp, sweet smell of earth, the prickle of November dawn—it was a comfortable feeling, and it was how I loved him.

Then there was the love I felt for certain soft-spoken teachers who made me think of other, richer places. There was the love I felt for girls who made my days (and nights) better just by being beautiful and having no control over what they did and said in my fantasies. There were kinds of love that didn't make sense. Love for food sometimes, a rising, bursting appreciation for the taste of venison or apples. There was the love of beautiful words, which came up in English class, a love I discussed with no one since I valued my reputation, what little I had. There was the love of finished tasks. The love of cracking knuckles, or a hot shower. The love of snow. The love of a shot deer. The love of a tree full of birds. The love of waking up, drifting off, dreaming.

And then there was the love I felt for Twila Flood—a love that felt the way her name sounded, like dusk and hard water. In this granite town, Twila was something unreal. Creature of decadent beauty. Too lovely to talk to. But I watched her. In the hallway. Walking past. Dark hair. Dark mouth. Twila. Hot. Silent. Swelling. Flood.

Which brings me back to Woodfern and the second thing it's famous for: the ice storm of 1988. It was the year Twila Flood was in my English class. I sat behind her where I could study the baby hair on the back of her neck, and a certain mole near her ear, and the glossy wave of her hair crashing on her shoulders. It was the year the school closed down overnight, with the students inside. It was the year a girl got pregnant in the halls of the school. It was the unfurling of my own embryonic understanding of love.

No one predicted the ice storm. It came suddenly and without warning while I was in Miss Little's English class, looking at Twila Flood's neck. I leaned toward her, longing to feel the heat off her body. She seemed nervous, biting her fingernails as if she were chewing herself out of a trap. I thought of the raw flesh under Twila's fingernails, pretty, unprotected. Outside, the light changed. The sky turned sickly, the clouds purple, gray and green, the colors of acid and bile.

"I love a storm," Ben Thomson said, running to the window just as the rain started: a whisper, snapping fingers, applause, boots up and down the stairs. Twila twisted in her seat to see out the window. Her cheeks were flushed with the natural warmth of her body. Kimberly Keenan crowded next to Ben at the window, and then other kids jumped up and joined them, shoving and crowding and watching the rain, until Miss Little ordered them all back to their seats.

Kimberly Keenan sat with voluptuous dignity. Kimberly gave the impression that she was bursting out of everything around her—chairs, clothing, her own skin. We boys had nicknamed her Deedee, as a tribute to her breasts, which were marvelously buoyant and seemed to defy both gravity and propriety. When we read *Their Eyes Were Watching God* in English class that year, I for one understood Hurston's description of Janie's pugnacious breasts. Not only her breasts, but Kimberly herself was pugnacious—and mean, and stupid. I didn't like her, but still I dreamed of her, being under and between and inside her—we all did— and if she had known the role she played in our masturbatory fantasies, I believe she would have been glad.

"I can see you as the puma," I said. "What would I be?" She glanced at me. "Maybe the moose?"

When class was over Twila got out of her seat and went to the window. I followed her, with no idea why I felt so brave. I stood behind her, where I could see her faint reflection in the window. Her hair was rich and dark. The bridge of her nose had an expensive fragility like the edge of a little saucer. Outside the air was silver with rain.

"Do you feel," Twila said, "that this is exactly what it will be like when the world ends? I mean ends again."

I opened my mouth, but I had exactly nothing to say.

"The flood," Twila said. She looked over her shoulder at me. "I'm not religious or anything," she said, "but I like thinking about the flood."

"Me too," I said. Not a lie because I figured *now* I'd think about it all the time.

"Do you ever feel like we're on the ark?" she said. "Like we're all the animals? And I'm some sort of wild cat. Like the puma?"

"The puma," I said. Her voice was intoxicating. She didn't belong here. She belonged in some rich and pristine place. A palace. A museum. "I can see you as the puma," I said. "What would I be?"

She glanced at me. "Maybe the moose?"

"The moose," I said. "The moose—in what way—?"

"I don't mean in the big and galloping way," she said. "It's more something about the nose or the eyes."

I put my hand on my nose.

"Not in the *big* sense of the nose," she said quickly. "I meant the *kindness* of the nose."

"Oh, the kindness," I said.

"Shit, now I offended you," she said. "I don't know what is wrong with me."

"Absolutely nothing," I said.

She turned away from the window in apparent disgust. "I like a storm, too," she said. "But my bus stop is a mile from my house. I'm going to get soaking wet."

Then she went into the hallway.

It occurred to me I could offer to ride the bus home with her and then *carry* her down the mile-long driveway, keeping her warm against my body. She could wrap her legs around my waist, and I could button my coat around both of us, and if she were chilled when we got home, I could give her a bath.

"It's turning to *ice*," Kimberly K. was yelling in the hallway. "It's half an inch thick!"

Ask anyone in town, they'll remember the ice storm. There were fourteen auto accidents in twenty-four hours; power was out for five days; six cows died of mastitis when their milk machines wouldn't run and their udders swelled to dangerous proportions. The school was shut down that night with the students inside. And worst of all, Kimberly Keenan's pregnancy, her doctor said, dated back to the night of the ice storm, leading me to imagine conception as an event as hard and perfect as ice, in which an implosion of matter inside the body forms, like the strands of an ice crystal, a precarious structure, made of bone, hair, and skin.

When we pushed out the school's front doors at 2:30, holding our backpacks to our chests, much the way I had earlier imagined holding Twila Flood, a wondrous transformation had taken place. The buses, benches, parking lot, and soccer field lay under a translucent layer of ice. In the yellow light, the ice had a brownish tint, like a beer bottle, and it was as smooth as if we'd made it in our freezers.

I watched everyone slipping and sliding down the front steps of the school. Twila Flood was as precise and graceful as the wild cat she imagined herself to be. I watched her climb onto her bus, which closed its doors with a sigh and crept into the icy parking lot. Then, in dreamy slow motion, it drifted sideways off the road, fishtailed across the soccer field, and hit a goal post. When the driver tried to move the bus again, the engine revved and the wheels spun madly and a smoky smell drifted across the field.

After that, Mr. Cupjik, our principal, herded everyone back inside. I hung back to make sure Twila got off that bus okay. From a distance I followed her inside. The kids from the runaway bus got to lie down in the library while they waited for the school nurse to check them over. The rest of us lined up outside the main office to call our parents.

"No one's going anywhere until we see what this storm's got planned," Mr. Cupjik said to us.

"So what are we supposed to *do*?" someone asked.

"Homework," Mr. Cupjik said.

"What about our parents?" someone else asked.

"They can pick you up if they want," Mr. Cupjik said. "That's their prerogative."

My mother answered the phone at my house.

"They're keeping us here," I said. "I don't even know how long."

"You want me to come get you?" she said.

"God no," I said.

"What are you going to do then? Stay there all night?"

"If I'm lucky," I said, thinking about Twila, the dark halls and the wind outside.

After the phone calls they corralled us into the gym. There were close to three hundred of us, and no one could sit still. Out the gym windows, we could see the bus like some strange dead beast in the field, already coated with a layer of ice.

They fed us the hotdogs meant for tomorrow's lunch. Miss Little herself handed them out. Then they tried to organize games: telephone and psychiatrist, but we refused to play. Mr. Cupjik and the chorus teacher began a round of "Hey Jude," but no one joined in.

Some parents came to take their kids. But by seven we could hear tree branches snapping under the weight of the ice, and no one else came. At nine the power lines came down and we were plunged into darkness. A roar went up in the gym. Mr. Cupjik opened the gym doors so the emergency lighting from the hallway would shine in. In that dim light, the faces around me seemed possessed with otherworldly spirit. A current of energy ran from kid to kid, a wild restless stirring. Their eyes were hard and black. Their lips glistened. I may have looked that way, too, but I didn't feel it. I found myself in a state of languor; around me, the wind howled musically and bodies drifted like figures in a dream. I set myself up in a corner of the gym, with my gym clothes bundled to make a kind of pillow.

"It's time to lie down," Mr. Cupjik announced at ten, and everyone laughed at this suggestion.

"Lie down on the floor and close your eyes," Mr. Cupjik said.

There were bodies everywhere, dark furtive figures prowling the shadows. They reminded me of wolves or thieves. They were in a kind of rapture. A kid climbed to the top of the bleachers and held his arms out so that in silhouette he looked crucified. Then more kids climbed up after him and huddled at the top, and they looked like bats, wings folded. Miss Little and the other teachers walked wearily in circles around the room, trying to keep everyone in one place.

Around eleven I went to the bathroom and found Ben Thomson and his girlfriend. Ben had her pinned to the wall. Her head rubbed up and down, her hair a halo of static. They went into the stall while I used the urinal. The faint thump thump of them against the door. Dim graffiti. *Suck me. Fuck me.* Water splashing in the sink.

In the gym, kids were finding where to go—into corners, behind gymnastics mats. Miss Little's flashlight poked into their darkness. They growled. Gnashed their teeth. The place got warm. Sweat. Crashing wind.

I lay back on my folded arms, listened to the bodies all around me, the cracking of branches outside. Drifting, dreaming. When all at once Twila Flood lay down beside me.

"Hello James," she said.

Twila Flood and I had been born one day apart in the same hospital, and I'd been comforting myself with this knowledge since the third grade, as evidence that Fate had thrown us together once and would certainly do it again sooner or later. I liked to think of us together as babies, her open round mouth, her soft wrinkled newborn body. I wondered if we had come from the same place, before being born.

And now seventeen years after we had lain together in bassinets, we were apparently going to lie together again. It looked for all intents and purposes as if she intended to sleep, or not sleep, right there next to me all night long.

"I don't know why my mom didn't come get me," Twila said.

"Roads," I said. Twila stared at me. Complete sentences, I told myself sternly.

"I would rather ice skate home than spend the night here," she said.

"A car could hit you," I said.

"I guess so," Twila said. She pushed up on her elbows and looked around the room. "Everyone is acting drunk. This is the only quiet place. Right here where you are."

My love for her flared unbearably.

"Do you want to lie against the wall?" I said. "It might be quieter."

"It's a difference of like three feet," she said.

"The wall might absorb sound?" I said.

"Anyway, I don't even do that at home," she said. "Lie against the wall, I mean. My bed's in the middle of the room."

"Oh, your bed," I said.

"Because I bump my elbows," she said.

"You must thrash around a lot."

"I guess I do," she said. "Plus I bruise incredibly easily."

She hiked up the sleeve of her sweater and showed me a purplish circle just above her elbow. It looked as soft as fruit.

"That's a good one," I said.

Twila wrapped her jacket around her like a blanket. She said, "I guess I'll try to get some sleep now," and she turned on her side, facing me, and closed her eyes.

I lay there a long time before I fell asleep that night. I heard the murmur of kids who didn't want to waste time sleeping. Behind Twila, I caught glimpses of dark shapes moving with purpose. I grew sleepy listening to the ice outside as it tore down telephone lines. I grew sleepy watching Twila as she slept. Her breath was long and slow, and long and low. Her hair, escaping from its rubber band, curled like some exotic underwater weed. I touched the tip, the tendril closest to me. She was so beautiful I was moved to sing, under my breath, the first two verses of "Is This Love" by White Snake. Don't fall asleep, I told myself, don't fall asleep. Lying on the hard gym floor, my heart, the blood within me, swelled with love.

For weeks all we heard about were damages from the ice storm. Trees, barns, and fences: destroyed by ice. My own house suffered, too. Four windows blown out and the chimney snapped like a pipe cleaner. Heat out all over town. Burst pipes. Horses, cows, dogs, and one old woman frozen to death. And Kimberly Keenan was pregnant.

When her father found out, he hit her in the face, avoiding her stomach so he wouldn't hurt the baby. She told him it wasn't her fault, but the school's, since she'd gotten pregnant there in the hallways. Mr. Keenan stormed into Mr. Cupjik's office the next day demanding to know what the hell the school was going to do about it. He'd had his doubts about the virtue of Woodfern High since last year when he'd opened his front door in the morning, and found Kimberly on the doorstep, passed out with her panties in her pocket. She'd been at a school dance the night before.

Kimberly didn't know who the father was; it was either, she admitted, a tenth grader named Simon or Brady Doyle, a senior basketball star who told us that Kimberly Keenan was "like a bank, men," a place to "deposit your dick and keep your cum."

"Guess you should have made a *withdrawal*," someone said.

"Funny," Brady Doyle said, flicking that kid on the nose.

Then he told us in detail where and how he'd had her. In girl's locker room, bent over a bench. Although I had often imagined scenes in the locker room in which it were I and not Brady Doyle holding Kimberly by the flesh of her bare hips, when Brady Doyle told us this, when he showed us with his hands exactly how he had bent her like a Barbie doll over the girl's locker room bench, I wanted to hurt him.

Once it was all out in the open, there was a buzz of rumors: Mr. Keenan was suing the school; Mr. Cupjik was the father of Kimberly's baby; Kimberly had been charging money the night of the ice storm, her new career sadly ruined before it even got off the ground due to the unforeseen pregnancy. To me the gossip seemed flat and dirty like the blackened snow that piled up on the side of the road.

The night of the ice storm had come to stand for everything I detested about myself. It was a night of squandered opportunities. What a night! everyone said. Relationships had been forged and consummated; conception had occurred! But did I act on my desires that night? Was I courageous? I did not and I was not. I slept. I dreamed. I lay down near my love and never once reached out for her.

And it soon became clear there would be no second chance. I didn't mean anything more to Twila after our night on the gym floor. She didn't turn around in English class to meet my eyes. When I passed her in the halls she said, "Hi James" and that was all. I couldn't believe how desperately I hung onto those careless words. In bed at night, I thought of Twila, but even in my fantasies, she was out of reach, and there was no relief for the desire I felt.

In February she started dating a boy named Bo, a jerk I'd known forever. I saw them kissing at the end of a hallway one afternoon. His hands ran down her back and came to rest on the upper curve of her butt, a gesture so familiar to her she apparently didn't even notice. It was terrible knowing that while I was still deluged with dreams of Twila Flood, she was opening up her soft inner parts to someone else; it was as if someone else had seen the pink underneath of her fingernails, the wrinkled newborn self I thought only I knew about. The love I felt for her, so wild and pneumatic for so long, was punctured suddenly and sagged inside me. It all seemed ruined, every sweet thought I'd ever had.

To keep from thinking about Twila, I thought about a possible life I might have someday far from here. At night in bed I pictured an imaginary city where I would one day live, the defining features of which were tall brick townhouses with window washers swinging off the walls like trapeze artists, women in high heels walking bejeweled dogs, and mustachioed hot dog vendors on cobblestone streets. I wore suits and hurried from place to place, constantly saying, "Keep the change." In a living room in this city, I worked late into the night, bent over a desk against a window illuminated by one lamp. Women walking by on the street could see me in that glow and they liked me. The women of this city were beautiful and lonely; their gorgeous feet ached at night. They lived in my neighborhood and hoped to run into me at the grocery store.

As far as I knew no one in my family had ever lived in such a city, or any city at all. They were vegetable farmers and granite men as far back as my great-great-grandfather, and not one of them had been to college. My mother had her own dreams for me, as did Miss Little, who seemed fixated all spring on my SAT scores and college applications, the education she saw spreading out in front of me like a golden staircase leading out of a pit of dirt.

To occupy my mind the spring after the ice storm, I read college brochures, brought my GPA up to a 3.8, and took practice SAT tests. Miss Little stayed after school drilling me on analogies and antonyms. I was happy for the extra work. I figured ambition is to anguish as salve is to infection. I began to think of college as the way to escape from gossip and dirty winter snow and dirty sex against the wall of the boys' bathroom, and poverty, and what I was born into, and who I was supposed to become.

In English class I didn't look at Twila Flood anymore; I gazed out the window instead. The spring sky was a thin membrane of blue, on it projected translucent wisps of possibility, a future that seemed always on the verge of ripping and floating away.

In July, Kimberly gave birth to a premature baby born without bones. It wasn't alive, but still I pictured its eyes blinking, small black stones in a jellyfish body. We heard that she cried and clutched the body until a kind nurse coaxed it away from her.

In August, I met a girl who worked at the movie theatre in Littleton. She went to a different high school, and apparently hadn't been part of the "we think of James as a *friend*" conspiracy I had suffered from for years. For a month, we went out every weekend. We went to keg parties on a dark golf course after midnight where the rolling green in the moonlight looked like silver, like money. We swam at Loon Lake, and I studied the summer kids up at their lake houses for the weekend. They lay in the sun like we did, they swam to the barge and dove off just like us, but these kids, up from Boston or New York, seemed to experience sensation more acutely than we did. When they lay in the sun, they soaked it up until they glowed. The water beaded on their skin like pearls. They were always yawning, stretching, rolling over with lazy pleasure. The girl from Littleton called them hedonists, a word that pleased me.

On Labor Day weekend, the last weekend before I began my senior year, we took a tent out to Woodfern Lake and found a place to set up camp among the old browning pines. While I drove the tent stakes into the earth, she built a fire. Later she followed me inside the tent, and we lay looking at one another until the campfire had sputtered down to red. We kissed. She twined her fingers through my hair. We exhausted ourselves kissing and I fell asleep with my mouth still on her. I woke a second later with the desperate impression that I was falling and had to hold onto her. I pulled her up on top of me and then she pulled me on top of her. In the dark I couldn't see her face but the heat and dampness from her body and her wet smell left me almost senseless.

I couldn't picture her face as I pushed and pushed against her until I slid in through the leghole of her underwear and found myself where I had so longed to be. She asked me to put on a condom and I managed to. Then I found my way inside her again, and in the quick and mindless dizziness that followed, my brain misfired, producing images of women I had never touched and pasting parts of them on parts of her. A lonely woman passing by my city window; Kimberly Keenan's breasts; my mother scratching my back; Twila. In the night the packed dirt under the tent became the hard gym floor and Twila Flood was the darkness that enveloped me.

Immediately afterwards, I flicked on my flashlight and looked down at the wet condom flapping off of me. I had done what I'd wanted to do, and I felt as shrunken and insignificant as ever. Now that my impulse lay in a little milky pearl in the tip of the condom, I felt small and scared and tender as a mole.

When I woke up, the sun was new and warm and orange through the tent. All around was the smell of latex and semen. My fingers smelled like the inside of her. In the sunlight I could see more of her than I wanted. I could see each pore on her face. I could see the hair follicles on her upper lip, and the pale hairs moving as she breathed.

I stepped out of the tent. The old shaggy pines were glowing, as if their needles had been polished. The earth looked rich and golden.

I remembered the morning after the ice storm when we emerged from the dark school, blinking like cave animals, and we saw what we had never seen before—each twig, each leaf, each blade of grass outlined in crystal. The school bus in the soccer field shimmered like some sort of wonderful statue, and the soccer field hurt our eyes with the splendor of sunlight glinting off it. I stood on the school steps, and searched out Twila Flood. Her hair was tangled, all caught up in knots on the back of her head. I would have liked to coax those tangles out for her, carefully holding her head with one hand. I felt that we were sharing something amazing, seeing how the ordinary world can be transformed overnight.

I packed up the tent, drove the girl home, and that night, I showed up at Twila Flood's house. We stared at each other over the threshold.

"You want to come in?" she said finally, and led me into her living room, where she'd been watching an old movie, a line of women dancing in costumes that sparkled.

Twila sat on the couch, and I went down on my knees beside her.

"I have to say something," I said. "You may think I'm crazy, but I have to say it."

"I do think you're crazy," she said. "Get the hell up."

She looked almost scared. Her eyelids were smudged with mascara.

"I'm pretty much in love with you," I said. "I've felt this way for a long time, and I've never said a word about it, because I didn't know if there was even the slimmest chance in hell you'd feel the same way, but I decided it was time to say something whether you feel it or not. I have to let you know, don't I?"

Twila Flood reached up and smoothed the hair at her forehead. She looked at me and touched her hair distractedly.

"This is a big surprise," she said finally.

"I know you're with Bo," I said. "I should probably leave you both alone."

"Bo and I broke up," Twila said.

"My god," I said and started to cry. I covered my face with my hands as if that would keep her from seeing. For a while we stayed just like that, Twila on the couch, me on my knees beside her, and behind us, women dancing, shimmering, making sharp sounds with their heels on a stage.

Then Twila pried my hands from my face and made me look at her.

I'd been saving up for a truck, and that fall I bought it so I could drive Twila home from school every day. I never got tired of seeing her in the passenger's seat although it gave me a feeling that was both happy and sad. It was the way I felt when I saw something beautiful that I knew wouldn't last, an upsurge of appreciation for something I was already grieving for.

I was different now, I told myself, from the boy who had fallen asleep the night of the ice storm. I was not a boy any longer, I thought. When it was time to kiss Twila Flood, believe me when I say I kissed her. The days swept by. I didn't want to stop and think. I rushed through the days so I could end up at her house, touching her. When we first made love Twila closed her eyes. I wanted her to look, to know it was me and no one else. I kept my mouth on her jaw when I came, sucking on the bone.

In the spring I was accepted to three of the four colleges I applied to. One was Northwestern in Chicago, and Miss Little waved the acceptance letter in my face telling me I was a fool not to go. She looked so angry, I wondered what was in it for her. She didn't have to stay here. She was from Connecticut and had gone to school in Boston. She had a big wealthy family elsewhere. She could leave anytime she pleased.

"I have a girlfriend," I said. "I have to think about her."

"Very noble of you," she said.

"I can't leave her," I said.

"Well you can't stay here," she said.

"You're here," I said. "You're staying here. How is that different?"

She looked at me over the top of her glasses and shook her head in disgust. She never answered me, but I figured it out anyhow. It was a rescue mission, Miss Little teaching at this school. She was here to find the worthy ones and take them out with her. I was her project. If I failed, she failed.

The next time we made love, it was afternoon but dark as night outside, a dirty April sky. The air was cold and sluggish, the ground covered with gray slush. I stopped moving and put my fingers on Twila's eyelids.

"Why don't you ever look at me?" I said. She opened her eyes.

"I'll look at you," she said, "if you want me to."

Later she said, "You know what I was thinking? I was thinking we could have a baby."

"What—you and me?" I said.

She snuggled up against me under the covers. Her naked arms around my chest were hot.

"What, like Kimberly Keenan?" I said. "Well, that's a great idea, Twila. Because she's a perfect model for how to live our lives."

"I didn't mean it like that exactly," she said.

I pulled away from her and sat on the edge of the bed, cold. She scrambled to pull the blanket over her naked body. I looked down at her and she looked up at me.

Her face looked small, like her mother's. Her mother had a narrow face, a pointy chin. Her mother was disappointed in how life had gone for her.

"Please don't look like that," I said.

"What do you mean?" Twila said.

"I'm sorry," I said. "I don't know what's wrong with me."

But I knew what it was. I was fighting the rising realization that Twila was just like everyone else in Woodfern. She was more lovely than the rest of them, that was true. But the expression on her lovely face was often remote as if she were refusing to exist in the beautiful world around us. I wanted her to be extraordinary. I wanted our love to be "wondrous strange" and sex to be a miracle. That it wasn't made me angry in a way I'd never known.

That night I stood on the back porch with my mother. We were chilly, but we stood there anyway, smoking cigarettes.

"How can I just give up going to college?" I asked my mother.

"You can't give it up," my mother said. "You have to go. The way it's supposed to work is that the children are supposed to do better than the parents. You have to do better so your children can do better. It's called evolution."

"Dad didn't go," I said. "He stayed here with you."

"That's different," she said. "He didn't ever want to go."

"Well there's no way I can leave her," I said, meaning Twila.

"You can come back for her," my mother said. It may have been the only lie she ever told me.

I had loved Twila Flood as long as I could remember, since the day she was born, if not before. When I held her I felt a tiny hot spot inside me, a raw sore the size of a seed, an inflammation. When I drove away in September, the spot blistered and burned, but a month later it had cooled, and a year after that it went completely cold, a little lump of clay.

"It doesn't matter," Twila said when I kissed her goodbye. "You would have left some day."

It didn't feel that way to me. For me there were two conflicting loves, each one clamorous and exacting. On the one hand there was the love I felt for Twila Flood, a love that felt the way her name sounded, like dusk and hard water. That kind of love can paralyze a person, drown them. On the other hand there was this new love I felt for a city I had never seen, a city of lonely women, brick steps, "half-deserted streets."

There was the James that I would become in that city, and I loved him resolutely. He had a duty to fulfill, improvements to make on the life his parents lived, so that his future children could do even better. He had to buy a suit. He had to learn to wear sunlight and lake water like jewelry. He had to climb out of here. It was a narrow escape. Thank God. He walked away. He didn't go back.

Once or twice in the new life I've come across kitchen countertops made from the pink and blue granite I recognize from home. I touch it. Smooth as ice, and cold, too. And from the depths of its mottled patterns comes rising one mislaid memory.

It's the spring of my senior year. Our new English teacher reads the last paragraph of *Brave New World* out loud. The men climb into the lighthouse. Feet hang down like compass needles. The swinging rope turns right then left. North, then east, then south, then west. Kimberly Keenan listens with terrible concentration. When it ends, she begins to wail. She stands up and cries in front of us, her mouth distorted.

We freeze. Mr. Hendricks casts around the room and his terrified eyes fall on me. He's trying to tell me something. This place is dangerous, he seems to say. Get out of here, he seems to say. Is that the moment I make my decision?

"My baby," Kimberly screams. Over and over, "My baby!" Her friends come and put their arms around her and lead her out into the hallway.

R. G. Evans
"And Then What America, And Then What?"

—MILTON KESSLER

What if California wasn't the end of possibility?
Gleaming out past Alcatraz and Coronado—
someplace real to reach, if only you could walk across the water.

Forget Manifest Destiny. What is ever manifest?
What is destined? Today is only lupine yesterday
wrapped up warmly in fresh wool.

Call it The Inevitable Bliss, or if you like,
call it Best Western, the place where they have
to take you in when Home turns you away.

What would you say to such a sunset,
to the glittering waves conjured by the moon?
I'll say I'm the brother of the water when I mean I'm the sister of the air.

What if we have always had this, this more-than-we-had-ever-imagined?
What if all this time we've lived in dread
of the end of something that just goes on and on . . .

and then what, America, and then what?

The Body, An Afterthought

FOR HAL SIROWITZ

The story says that first God worked the clay,
  a dirty little doppelganger, and *then* he gave it life—
    but what kind of genius is that?

Surely he had something up his sleeve
  before he hunkered down in the dust
    to shape such punitive bodies as these.

Maybe, like a firefly he'd caught
  by pure dumb luck alone,
    it hovered over his clean, cupped hands—

a will-o'-the-wisp, a tempest with no teapot,
  lightning that never dreamed of the bottle
    that could hold it. To lock it up,

he sculpted a cell out of the earth, and just before
  the tides he made could wash the sands away,
    he got down on his knees and blew

his shiny gewgaw up the waiting nostrils of its prison.
　　　　And God saw that this was *good*? Listen—
　　　　　　　is that a tin cup rattling these rib cage bars,

a voice crying, *Can anybody hear me?*
　　　　I swear I can do this forever—
　　　　　　　can anybody hear?

Thomas Reiter
Mathew Brady at Gettysburg

He comes out from under his camera's hood.
Before the shutter could take depth of field,
July 2, 1864, the first anniversary
of the battle for Little Round Top,
something rose out of the earth
that would surely ghost the exposure.

Cicadas. Mathew Brady shoulders his tripod.
The color of fox-marks on an old page,
seventeen years underground and now
they're climbing trees where snipers hid
beside the pools and meanders of Plum Run,
ground the 5th Texas and the 44th Alabama took
though every charge up Little Round Top
was broken. He studies how skin
casings open like pods, how adults
struggle free, eyes like blood blisters.

Their song's a ripsaw and a plank
though girth and short legs alone make them
the tenors of this requiem ground.

July 5, 1863, he arrived
in his darkroom wagon too late, the dead
already buried. But he would not
dress his assistants in uniforms
and strew them about as some were doing,
then back date the photographs.
No amateur theatrics could testify.

As their mica wings dry, cicadas fill the air.
They land on his broad-brimmed hat
and linen duster as though he's strolling
through a peaceable kingdom. They move
upslope toward the Union breastworks.
A senator has commissioned him
to document the ground where the 20th Maine
held the left flank of the Union line
at Little Round Top and his son died.

But now cicadas have the field.
Bending to a nipple of granular earth
nymphs are still pouring from, he thinks,

Lord, the blood must have fed them
as they molted. If I only had
a camera to give that to the world!

Makeshift graves for Federals and Confederates
alike where they fell. He remembers
a print in his gallery exhibition
The Dead at Antietam that grown men
wept to see. The 9th New York's color bearer
was found draped over a boulder
so he's going sideways into his first grave,
joints and muscles locked—Who would break them?—
as though lying spoon-fashion with his love.
Antietam, Shiloh, the Wilderness.
He smiles now that he once told a journalist
"A voice in me said *Go*, and I went."

How many here were never reburied,
he wonders, their wooden markers
washed away by the squalls of July 4, Lee
in retreat? History? Tomorrow this hatch

will tunnel back into home ground,
and two emergences from now Mathew Brady
will die in a charity ward, most of his 10,000
glass negatives gone to build greenhouses.

Yes, here's the standpoint.
He positions himself beside Plum Run
—cicada shells are flowing by—
where Alexander Gardner, his rival
in *Harper's Weekly,* took the only
photograph he has ever envied:
the 15th Alabama's chaplain lies
face-up among cinnamon fern, one hand
washed by the shallows glinting like tassels
on a colonel's sash, the other raised in rigor.
God's blessing on the least of creatures.

Boy on Market Day
(St. George's, Grenada)

He machetes raw cane for you,
sweet as any candy cane; he opens
a coconut and inserts a straw.
His grandmother sits at a folding table,
cash box on her lap. Around her
in the stall, cut flowers and fruit and crafts
in baskets of woven palm fronds.
On the table she's arrayed
plates of spices that flavor her preserves:
vanilla pods, nutmeg, essential oil
of cinnamon. After the exhaust
from overloaded jitneys you'll bend to these
and to jasmine, bird of paradise,
heliconia and Joseph's coat.

When she turns the handle of a music box
playing *Yellow Bird*—they're kits from Miami
she assembles—he averts his eyes.
He watches a frigate bird
high over the harbor seize a crab
or fish from a seagull and disappear

behind the battlements of Fort George.
His father, who once told him
the sea waits at the horizon
to take on all comers, he's outbound
on a schooner carrying root crops.
His mother is boiling clothes in their yard.

By mid-afternoon, the market closed,
he'll be running along the sea wall
past Cable & Wireless and Duty Free,
past rum talk and laughter from Mama Vi's
three chairs around an oil drum.
At the old airport a Cuban DC-3
hit by an American gunship
exploded, and twenty years after Urgent Fury
the wreckage is still there.
You'll see him at the anchorage
wheeling and wheeling with a stick
the scorched frame of a passenger window
that now he zigzags to keep upright,
that now he can barely hold back.

His own horizon keeps to itself.
He sells you custard apples, christophene,
passion fruit, and Look: a hat
his grandmother wove, leaves
of a breadfruit tree descended from
a sapling brought here by Captain Bligh.

Paul Ruffin
Hi-Ho, Hi-Ho, Off To The Gun Show We Go

BILLY WAYNE TAKES IN THE GUN SHOW

Lest there be some confusion with the living or the dead, I have changed the names of the people in this piece—instead of using Willard, the actual name on the fellow's coveralls and tattoo, I have used Billy Wayne, and the girl's name on the tattoo has been changed from Tammy to Lynelle; to be extra safe, I have changed the flower color on the tattoo from violet to orange. Newspapers are very sensitive about the use of actual names and descriptions in pieces when there is some vague suspicion that the columnist might be telling an unkind truth.

Billy Wayne knows only that what he's holding in his hand is a gun that was probably made long before he was born and is likely to rust away to nothing before he ever reads a book. He is in fact holding a Martini-Enfield, made famous by British troops during the Anglo-Zulu War of the late nineteenth century, but it is not a fact that concerns him—he is disturbed that the chamber is too large for a .410 and too small for a twenty gauge, and every military cartridge he knows anything about slides way down into the bore. In short, Billy Wayne cannot shoot his gun, and this troubles him no end. What if someone charged his trailer?

His name is sewn in white on a dark blue oval patch on the back of his coveralls, which are a dark-striped lighter blue with old and new grease smudges on them, which means, I 'spect, that he does not work in management. In a burst of charity I will assume that his name is on his back so that others will know what to call him, or so that he can tell his coveralls from someone else's, should he for some reason leave them hanging somewhere. For self-identification he needs merely to glance at the tattoo on his wrist, where his name is emblazoned on a blue ribbon that threads through the fangs of a large-mouthed snake wreathed in vines with orange flowers dotting them. A smaller ribbon, pink, with *Lynelle* on it, dangles from the snake's lower jaw. I have spent enough time in the halls of academe that I should be able to decipher the symbolism, but Billy Wayne would have to be still awhile for me to do it, and it takes a special need to ask someone with a gun—especially someone who looks like him—to hold still while you study his arm.

I want to tell him about the rifle, but the tall man dressed in khaki he's talking to, before whom a table ripples with lever-action Winchesters on blue velvet, is doing it for me, patiently explaining that the Martini will not accommodate any cartridge that Billy Wayne has ever seen and that if by chance one did lodge in the chamber within striking distance of the firing pin, to pull the trigger on it would probably be supreme folly. Understanding man that he is, he does not phrase it this way to Billy Wayne. He puffs up his cheeks, holds his hands to them, then expels the air with an explosive sound, carrying his hands out as wide as he can fling them, suggesting that his fingers might be disconnected pieces of Billy Wayne's face—nose, ears, eyes, lips, etc. Billy Wayne nods *unh-hunh* and moves on down the line, where eventually I lose sight of him. If the Martini did not look like it had been used to drive steel fence posts in bad weather, he might well sell it.

My bet is that Billy Wayne will end up trading his tortured Martini and a hundred dollars for another exotic, say a Russian Nagant revolver with machining so crude you can file your fingernails or saw through jail bars with it and is currently selling for $65 through *Gunlist* and *Shotgun News*. He will take it home and try to fit .38 Specials into it, and if that won't work—and it won't, not by a long shot—he'll hang it on a wall for show or use it to weight a trotline, which is what he should have done with the Martini. But that's Billy Wayne's problem, not mine. Then, too, I could be wrong about the outcome. Anything can happen here.

Billy Wayne, along with a few thousand other souls, is at the gun show in the old Astrohall (now Reliant Hall), where several times a year the Houston Antique Gun Dealers Association holds its big fling, one of the largest in the country. These dealers are not out to skin anybody, but neither will they turn down a hide if it's handed to them. They are only human, no matter how the media and gun-control people might argue otherwise.

I have pounded the concrete aisles for four hours, enough time to examine only a third or so of the more than two thousand tables—laden with guns, clips (magazines, if you prefer), reloading tools and components, knives, and books—spread out in rows across the hall. It is a two-day job if done properly.

At the moment I am sitting high in a plush chair (as plush as they get here—all the others are folding metal) grading a paper and scribbling notes while my shoes are being shined. They are work shoes, I have told the shine man, but he says that he will put a high gloss on them, no matter what. They will look like polished *work* shoes, I tell him, but he smiles and whirls his brush and rag. With un-forked tongue I can say that I do not care what they look like when he's through, anymore than I cared what they looked like when I came in. I am in his chair and paying five dollars for a shine so that I may rest the feet inside those shoes. I've already timed him, and it takes twelve to fifteen minutes for him to get the shine he wants. With these shoes, maybe twenty. Whatever, it's worth the five dollars. I have advised him that I will give him another five for a different kind of Martini, one with an olive in it.

"Not at the gun show," he says, smiling. "Unless you want to go with me out to the truck, where I gots some shonuff white lightnin.'"

I decline.

When I'm through here and the shine man asks me to make room for the next customer, I'm going over into the antiques section of the hall to browse—that's where the women hang out while the men prowl the gun show aisles—and maybe find something interesting. (I am eclectic in taste.) Who knows, Lynelle might be over there, not that I would know her from any other woman, unless she's got a tattoo that says Billy Wayne on it. I could always yell out *Lynelle* and duck, see who turns. But such nonsense is chancy at a place like this, with ol' Billy Wayne walking around shouldering a Martini club. Besides, Lynelle is probably two thousand miles away from here, married to a manager, and has forgotten all about the fool who put her name on a tattoo, if she ever knew him.

BORAM

I decided that the name Rambo for our Macho Man might be a little hackneyed, so I changed it to Boram, pronounced Bow-Ram. *It does sound supercharged with testosterone, doesn't it, the bow and ram being ancient instruments of war? Further, it sounds biblical, even apocalyptic. (No confusion with bowhunters is intended.)*

Another time and place, armed as he is with a brace of pistols and something that looks like an Uzi dangling from a sling, folks would dive for the nearest cover to hide until Boram shambled away to another county. For this is, as they say in the movies,

He looks like an Anglicized, modernized Pancho Villa: broad and ponderous of stature, eyes cold gray balls of steel swinging back and forth in their slits, blond mustache constantly atwitch like some animal testing the wind.

one bad dude, not a man to mess with. He looks like an Anglicized, modernized Pancho Villa: broad and ponderous of stature, eyes cold gray balls of steel swinging back and forth in their slits, blond mustache constantly atwitch like some animal testing the wind. His hair has been shorn to short stubble, and the back of his head has a broad-lipped meaty smile between the crown and shoulders, perhaps somewhere on the neck; I cannot be certain where his neck begins and ends, but I can tell you its color. The back of his head smiles more than the front. I am reminded of the back of the head of a football coach I hated in high school—one night at the fair I flung half a candied apple right toward the middle of his tailgate smile. (It is better not to name him, since he might still be dangerous.) I pretended it was a grenade but did not wait around to hear it explode.

Boram wears camelflogged (I really do know the proper spelling) pants, bloused above scarred black combat boots, and an olive T-shirt that has printed on the front his solution for the world's undesirables: *Kill 'em all and let God sort 'em out.* He is not thinking about fire ants and mosquitoes. On the back he has worried out in black magic marker the words *White Power* and beneath that the letters *AB*, which could stand for *Aryan Brotherhood* or merely serve as evidence that he has made some initial progress in his attempt to learn the alphabet.

The pistols—which look like a Colt 1911 and Beretta, though like cars these days it's hard to tell at a distance—are held in place by the same belt that keeps the upper part of his belly from avalanching and compounding his more than ample middle. The little submachine gun, I'd hope semiautomatic, just looks *mean*. He carries a nylon bag on the opposite side from the sub; I doubt that it bulges with bibles or knitting.

He may be selling, he may have just bought, or he may simply be on parade, dressed bad, dressed to kill, to have his day, the only place he can do it without someone calling the police.

The men in blue at the door are supposed to have determined that he has no ammunition on board, and they have run little plastic ties between the frame and hammer of the pistols and through the receiver on the sub; so, if you like, you may make an obscene gesture at him and not fear a riddling from his heavy metal. But there is the question of what's in his bag (un-deactivated grenades? a clutch of charged magazines?) and always the wide parking lot to cross afterwards, so I keep my tongue in my cheek and my finger where it belongs. Sticking out your tongue or flinging him a finger could be an easy suicide, as certain a way as any, perhaps swifter and more resolute than to unfurl a finger in Houston traffic.

This is a man who longs for Armageddon, who has plotted many times over the scenarios he will follow when, as the poet Yeats put it, the center cannot hold and "anarchy is loosed upon the world, / The blood-dimmed tide is loosed . . ." It is coming, the blood-dimmed tide, he has told himself, and he will make it through, he will *survive*. He hopes only that when things give way, he will be at his trailer home, mobile and ready to haul to the mountains. I am only guessing here, but I can imagine it bristling with guns of every sort, so that should the enemy be a cool, distant speck on the landscape or a hot savage breath upon him, he will have the proper weapon. I can even fancy a rotating turret on the roof, a fifty-caliber barrel protruding from it trained on the horizon.

As he shuffles down the aisles glancing right and left, the stream of people parts for him, flows to either side, joins again behind, some looking back and grinning and rolling their eyes, others intent on their business. Boram makes the corner to stalk another aisle, and I lose sight of him in the crowd.

Perhaps I have been unkind to this fellow. For some mother brought him into this world and still loves her big boy, pinches his cheeks, coos over him as she serves his favorite dessert. He is yet the apple of her eye. It may be that he is as gentle to the core as the pudge he was at three, jostling on his father's knee and drooling. In another gush of Christian charity let us believe this of him in closing: that he is a Jesuit in training, a gentle peacemaker playing a role to help him better understand the people he fancies he may someday be called on to minister to, assuaging their fears, soothing their savage spirit.

THE WOMEN OF THE GUN SHOW

Most of the people at the gun show are ordinary *men*, sensible and sane and conservative to moderate in their political leanings. Some hunt, some collect, some target shoot, some reload; some do all of these; but like gun-control advocates, they would keep guns out of the hands of those who would misuse them and insist on severe punishment for those who commit a crime with a firearm. And they cringe at the prospect of a world roamed by Rambos, whom they would have caged and fed daily a ration of carrots and cabbage and Prozac. Businessmen, professors, carpenters, doctors, lawyers, butchers, bakers, candle-stick makers (fairly rare these days)—they are all there, looking and touching and buying often enough that the dealers keep coming back. I go because I like to look at the guns and study the people. It's the cheapest entertainment I can mention in the paper.

Man's world though the gun show may be, a few women roam the aisles, almost always with their boyfriends or husbands, sometimes pushing babies in buggies, and women women tables. (I must assume that if a man mans a table, a woman *womans* it.) Even behind the table, though, the woman is usually with her husband or live-in, her counter-gender (pun intended).

Viewed by ravening feminists, the women of the gun show compliantly follow in the wake of their men like hollow shells adrift in their wake. "It is in their blood and brains to do it, these weaker ones," they would say with contempt. "They do not have the backbone to resist. They would follow their men into hell."

And gun show women would answer, "It's none of your business, but sometimes we *do* follow them into hell. Or halfway there. And we will again and again. It makes the going easier for them, and more often than not we can drag them back. Those who came before us, generations ago, followed them across the great water and over mountains and through swamps and rivers, fire and flood, wherever they wanted to go. We follow them, as we always will, no matter their purpose or passion, for we know that without us the world would plunge into chaos by morning. And let me add, you constipated bitch, at least I have a man."

No man has made them come here. No arm has been twisted. They come by choice. And this choice is dictated by common sense. They are, in fact, guardians of the financial realm, moderators of male passion for guns and knives and swords; they temper the appetite for ordnance (*ordnanism*, if you will). Without these calm heads along, the men would walk out with truckloads of guns, taking out second and third mortgages, signing promissory notes running well into the next century, and putting up the titles to their trucks and cars.

Hefting this nice Winchester '73, holding it out at arm's length, our typical husband says, "Lord, just look at it, Honey. Can't you just see that hanging on the wall above the mantle?"

"No, I can't, Jack," the wife answers. "What I can see is $1200 worth of furniture for the den that mantle is in. Gallery's running a sale on oak."

"I've always wanted one of these. It's in NRA excellent condition, bore's almost mint. Just look down that bore." He has dropped the lever and inserted a bore light.

"No woman wants to look down the barrel of a gun, Jack. Talking *about* a bore. You look down the bore if you want to, and then put the gun back." She may even be secretly surprised at the rhyme.

"But the price is right, Sweetheart. Look at the *lines*."

"Think *bottom* line, Jack. Look at the *line* of Modine's teeth when we get home. Half her upper teeth have never met them on the bottom. They're like two benches full of strangers in her mouth. You and me never got braces, but she's going to have them."

"I got a little bit of extry money coming in from that valve job down in Bay City—"

"Little bit is right. Where's the other half coming from? The den furniture or the down payment on Modine's teeth is where. Just look at the gun, Jack, *feel* of it. Then put it back down on the velvet, where it really looks nice. You don't want to leave a gap on the man's table."

"Ma'am," the dealer says, springing to his feet, "I got three more—"

The look she gives him would freeze dry dirt. He shrugs and sits back down, staring at his hands.

"Hold it, Jack. Feel it and look at the pretty thing. Then put it back on the table. We don't need that gun."

He lifts and aims the rifle, works the lever, admires once again the fine craftsmanship that went into the walnut and steel, then lays it on the table and turns away, eyes wistful. She squeezes his arm, tiptoes, kisses him on the cheek. She has led him once again out of temptation.

Without his woman along, Jack would have bought the Winchester, den furniture and Modine's teeth be damned. And he would have faced unholy hell when he got home with it. There would have been an appalling fight with his mate that might or might not have known any reasonable bounds—he could have found himself later that night with a wad of blankets in the back of his pickup and that cold darling Winnie Chester to sleep with.

The women of the gun show fascinate me. I watch them sometimes, the pretty and the plain, and wonder what goes through their heads as they slowly walk the aisles beside their men, what they are dreaming of, what lines they are rehearsing to head off the next attempt to buy. This is not their tea—bag, cup, or crock. Their eyes declare the same dreadful boredom I used to feel in Foley's or Dillard's when I tagged along with my wife shopping for women's clothes. Though tedium settles over their faces like dust by mid-afternoon, in their eyes I see a scintilla of hope, like sunlight behind heavy clouds. They know that no vigil is eternal, no pain goes on forever.

Martin Jude Farawell
Gleaming

HOW HAPPY THEY SEEM
EVEN ON ICE, TO BE TOGETHER, SELFLESS,
WHICH IS THE PRICE OF GLEAMING.
—MARK DOTY, "A DISPLAY OF MACKEREL"

It's not about wanting to be special.
We know we aren't special. We want
Anonymity. Attention makes us
shiver. You know the feeling:
all your girl cousins laughing
as your nana gushes, "Who knew
you'd look so handsome in a uniform?"
We aren't thinking of ourselves, but only
of our work. For once, who we are
doesn't matter.
                          Doubt, anxiety, fear
mean nothing once you've put aside
your petty ego. We know that we
are part of something
bigger than ourselves,
a sea of people
who think and move as one
the instant we put on
those armbands.
It's how the Christian soldiers must have felt
marching on Jerusalem.

The Search for Atlantis

The heart   has its own   lost cities,   submerged
in the bruised green light   of memory.   What calls you
comes from there.   Is heard   between the waves,
an almost singing   wind   sometimes breathes
through a ravaged shell.   Or so you comfort yourself,
saying,   "Only wind.   Empty shell."
Rationalize   the keening   in the salt reeds,
the accusation   of a laughing gull,
until you're certain   that you don't   hear
what you hear,   know   that there is—
Yes.   There it is again.   Is it
a human voice?   Listen

                              to the sirens
and they will sing you   out of this life.   You will
go drowning toward the distant windows
of a vanishing city,   believing   this time   the past
will welcome you.   Sometimes   it seems   you've passed
your life   walking   underwater. Not quite
attached   to the earth. The atmosphere   unbreathable.
And even though you learned   an alien grace,

there was always   this body   to remind you
you did not belong.   And so,   you remain
lost   in your study   of the lost
and loved   —whole cities   that were
that never were—   when all the while,   just above,
is the world   you were born for.

Opportunity

This land, its bounty: We have been blessed.
To save it for our children: a sacred trust.
Awe and gratitude   are not enough.
There are strangers   who would take
what God placed here   for us.

The soft and weak   can afford to be sanctimonious
old women,   proud of their own
complaisance,   as long as they have us.
Heart, stomach: They lack what it takes
of both, to do   —to even want to know—
what we do.   They love their temples.
It's only temple guardians   they despise.

Cruelty?   They hate to admit a taste for it
is bred or beaten   into those like us.
They call their condescension   open-mindedness.
Until you have no choice,   you cannot know
the act of will required   to kill, to kneel,
to take and eat   a human heart.

Our Enemies Send Other People's Children on Missions of Suicide and Murder

Sautéing almost melt-away-tender livers,
the flesh eaters can't stop talking
about love
of duty and selflessness
the way you and I might
about peanut butter cookies
or Reuben sandwiches.

Despite their immense heads
and great strength
they don't like to use force,
they tell you
as their hands
weigh down your shoulders
like boulders of meat.

They want you to know
you're not alone,
they understand the courage required
to eat your young.

"Take heart," they say,
offering you one
wrapped in bacon.
"The future looks bright"
as the bonfires ahead
of tiny rib cages.

Huan Hsu
Tennis Mom

A few minutes after crossing over Narragansett Bay, I hear the deep breathing of a boy waking up.

"Sweetie, do you have your shoes on?" I say, sneaking a quick look over my shoulder.

"Yeah," Danny calls from the backseat. He takes a swig from his battered red water jug. The ice cubes, still there after two hours in the car, clack against the hard plastic.

I glance at his face in the rearview and smile. "We're almost there. Are you nervous?"

"Mo-*om*." His sleepy eyes widen in exasperation as he turns to look out the window. "Maybe a little," he whispers to the mansions drifting by like icebergs, their full weight looming behind giant trees, ivy-covered walls, long, cobblestone drives with gated entryways.

"You'll do fine, honey," I say. "Just have fun." Tempted to keep talking, I force myself to be quiet. I take a right onto America's Cup and look for Bellevue Avenue.

This is the farthest we've traveled for a tennis tournament in all of Danny's short career, and this is easily the biggest tournament he's ever played, not in terms of size, but prestige. Three weeks ago he won our town tournament, the East Hartford Boys Twelve and Under Championship, beating the best players in the area, and boosting his ranking high enough to get consideration for tournaments like the one today. Right after his new ranking appeared, he called the U.S. Tennis Association for a national tournament schedule, and since then has memorized all the requirements for a national ranking, selection to the New England Zonal team, and acceptance to the Super National Hard Courts, the Copper Bowl, Easter Bowl, Orange Bowl, and National Opens, none of which are mutually exclusive and all of which require airfare, hotel stays, chaperones, and charge entry fees that cost more than everything in Danny's bag right now.

The morning seems so long ago, but we're still in the middle of it. Driving through the estates of historic Newport adds to the disorientation. I slipped out of bed this morning at six, quietly but still waking Stan, who hasn't worked since getting passed over for tenure eight months ago, and who hasn't gotten up in time to take Danny's little brother, Tom, to soccer for almost as long. Down the hall and into the boys' room, I tiptoed past Tom, whose turn it is to play goalie for the Comets today, and pulled Danny from under his racecar sheets. Downstairs, everything was exactly where we laid it out last night, and I went over the directions again. Danny changed into his clothes in the living room while I cooked him an omelet, peeking out of the kitchen to check for hair under his arms or on his chest. He ate with his head cradled in his right hand and I ran next door to leave a note for Mrs. Van Gelder, asking if she could please drive Tom to his game, again. We were in the car at six-thirty and at the Hertz by quarter of, as I mentally checked off everything we needed to bring. Danny was wedged into the corner of the rental car's backseat by seven, the hood of his sweatshirt pulled low over his head, swaying with the road. I realized then that I had forgotten his pillow.

At the top of the hill, I make a right, and an enormous Victorian cottage appears. The Newport Casino is by far the nicest tennis club I have ever seen. What strikes me is not its size, but its permanence. Even the most posh facilities in the greater Hartford area seem like they were built in a few days and, if necessary, could be loaded up on a truck and moved someplace else. The Casino looks as if it has always been here.

The man at the desk points us to the courts, and we walk through a maze of mahogany and brass, leather chairs and couches clustered for conversation, huge oil portraits that reach up toward the high ceilings, newspapers and Tiffany lamps on muscular end tables. The sun swirls in thick glass windows set into even thicker walls. Stepping out onto the patio, I've never seen tennis courts look so natural on the land. We walk around a horseshoe-shaped piazza surrounding a single grass court, bright white chalk on green that seems to glow, then along the low wood fences that ring other grass courts on our way to the hard courts in the back. I think I hear waves breaking.

I catch up to Danny at the pro shop, a gazebo with several smooth coats of whitewash. He is staring intently at the wall.

"How does it look?" I ask.

He chews his bottom lip as he talks. "I play the number-one seed. Jay Goldman." He taps the draw and I stoop to read it. Someone was considerate enough to post it at the eye level of an eleven-year-old.

I don't know Jay, but I've heard of him, as every mother of a twelve-and-under in New England probably has. His name or picture is usually in the newsletters Danny gets from the USTA. In addition to being the number-one ranked twelve-and-under in New England, Jay also has a national ranking. And despite being the same age as Danny, Jay started playing fourteen-and-unders this summer. Danny told me that you're allowed to do this once it's obvious you're no longer being challenged in your regular age group. I asked him how someone could know if he wasn't being challenged anymore, but I only earned myself a pitying look.

Everyone knows the Goldman story. I first heard it from Donna Bright, the mother of Ned, a boy with whom Danny takes lessons. Anne Goldman is the daughter of Brazilian aristocrats who moved to Newport when she was young, and between the parties and ski vacations she became the number-one ranked junior in the country. She turned pro after graduating from Harvard, winning three college championships along the way, and reached something like fifteenth in the world at one point. Having traveled and won all she wanted in tennis, having lived an entire life in twenty-seven years, she retired still young and beautiful and began another. She started teaching at the Casino, where she met and then married Philip Goldman, as in Goldman Sachs. I shake my head whenever Donna tells me this story, and think about how much I still had left to do at twenty-seven—start my dissertation, sign for more loans, find a one bedroom.

I've been told to watch out for Anne if I ever have the misfortune of meeting her, that she's pretty horrible, the epitome of a tennis mother—quick tempered, over involved, win at all costs, and suffering from an enormous sense of entitlement. The stories circulate like Danny and Tom's video games. Like how she got the local USTA guy fired when he refused to make an exception for her missing an entry deadline, or how she reschedules Jay's matches so he can play them on their home court, or that the three new amendments in the New England section's rulebook were added as direct reactions to Anne's abuse of the original ones.

"I wonder why he's playing here," I wonder aloud, catching myself too late.

"Why wouldn't he?" Danny wrinkles his nose.

"Well, ah, I wasn't sure if he was good enough for this tournament."

Danny smiles, but his eyes tell me he's still thinking about my remark.

"Lucy!"

I turn around and Elaine Powell extends her arms for a hug. Her adorable son, Mark, hovers close to her side. The Powells live in New Haven, and Danny and Mark meet each other in tournaments often enough for Elaine and I to have become acquainted. I like Elaine. She's too oblivious and friendly to be a tennis mom. Mark and Danny strike up a nervous conversation. They look funny standing next to each other, Danny all knees and elbows, shoulders pulled up and head hunched over, almost a half-foot taller than Mark, a little lion with the perfect proportions of a miniature adult. Donna says that he needs to start growing if he's going to go anywhere in tennis, that even though Danny and Ned might lose now because of their awkwardness, they'll be the ones going to Zonals once they grow into their bodies. I think Mark is fine the way he is.

"Hi, Mrs. Campbell." Mark smiles shyly, dark eyebrows curving on his round face.

I ask him whom he's playing.

"Evan Schenk. He's from Nantucket. My mom had to tell me because I couldn't see the draw." His smile grows lopsided and he playfully smacks his head. "Man, I gotta start growing." My heart melts.

Elaine wishes us luck and Mark scoots off towing a jumbo-sized racquet bag. I hear a voice call for Dan Campbell, and I follow my son to a large white tent, stepping around the parents and bags and racquets and towels and water bottles and baby siblings that litter the patio. A tall, tanned older gentleman with a salt and pepper moustache stands behind the desk and a handsome college kid sits on a corner, one muscled leg on the ground while the other dangles with the confident laziness that I've only seen in athletes and cats. White sport shorts cling to their narrow waists and white polo shirts with little crocodiles hang perfectly on their shoulders. A white sweater drapes around the kid's neck like a girlfriend. They chat with a blonde woman wearing tight white linen pants slung low on her flat stomach, a thin white blouse open to her chest, and her son, a boy with perfect teeth and the sinewy build of an old fisherman. The collar of his unbuttoned polo shirt stands up, as if he had just slipped off a blazer and tie; a bleached Groton baseball cap is slapped on his head. All of them practically shine. I look like I dressed in the dark, which I did.

Danny waits at the top of the path while the college kid gives the boy a can of balls. They slap hands and laugh about something, then the boy brushes past Danny and leads the way to the court next to the pro shop. I fight the urge to hug Danny or fix his hair or rub his shoulders, and give him a quick nod, a tough, upward flick of my head, like the way the boys greet their friends. For this, I get a grin. I'm learning.

The boys go through the gate and it clinks shut. I pull out a chair at a wrought iron table and set my things down on its heavy glass top. A young girl in a white polo shirt appears, opens the shade, and vanishes.

I uncap a red pen and take a paper off the stack I brought with me. Danny's matches are usually a good chance for me to catch up on my grading, and I've become good enough to do it and still see the important points of each game. Newport has score cards on every court, so I don't have to work as hard to keep track of the match. Against Jay's serve, Danny wins the first three points and after a long rally, wins the game on a shot that hits the net and just drops over on Jay's side. The boys are taught to hold up a hand and apologize for lucky shots like that, something I always appreciated about tennis, and one of the reasons I let Danny pursue the sport despite the warnings of the Comet parents, some of whom quickly steered their children to soccer after bad experiences with tennis. But I like tennis' emphasis on sportsmanship, how the handshake after the match isn't just a tradition, but a rule.

After the ball lands, Danny makes a fist and jogs over to the white park bench next to his pile of equipment. He plops down and takes a drink from his jug, squinting as he tilts his head back. He's only on the other side of the court, but seems so distant, as if I'm looking at him through the thick glass of an aquarium.

I shake my pen to get his attention. "Danny, do you need more water?" I call. After watching in horror as boys threw up and passed out from dehydration during the last tournament, I've become a bit of a nag. He waves his hand quickly, pushing me away.

"You know, you better be careful about talking to your son." The blonde woman has taken her time walking to the court, and now she speaks, measured and unaccented, as she passes behind me. She smoothes her thighs before sitting down a few yards away, shoulders back, regal but relaxed, and crosses her toned legs. Without makeup, and her wavy hair almost reaching her waist, she seems both former tomboy and glamazon. I shift in my seat and tug at the hem of my shorts. "Oscar will get on you real quick if he thinks you're trying to coach your son," she says. Oscar must have been the older man, Oscar Davies. His name is usually in the USTA newsletters along with Jay's. He coaches players on the professional tour, and, according to Donna, any kids who want to work with him have to pass through an extensive screening process.

Donna's my main source of information about the tennis circuit. She tells me what's going on, when the club starts a new session, which tournaments Danny should

I wonder why "tennis mom" has such a bad connotation. Then again, I've never seen soccer moms make their children cry or slap them during a game.

sign up for, what equipment the kids use these days. Ned and Danny are about the same age and started taking lessons at the same time. In the beginning, Donna and I would wait for our sons together and laugh at our ignorance. It was refreshing to know that I wasn't the only one who didn't have a clue. Donna, however, had time to learn the ropes. Her husband runs a private medical practice and she shuttles Ned and his sister Emma to their activities. Now she likes to joke that she's a full-blown tennis mom.

I wonder why "tennis mom" has such a bad connotation. Then again, I've never seen soccer moms make their children cry or slap them during a game, like one mother did after her son lost the first set to Danny. Soccer moms don't start fights with other parents, tournament directors, or officials. They don't try to change game times to accommodate birthday parties, school dances, or trips to the Cape. They don't fake injuries for their kids in order to protect their rankings. But I don't, either, and I imagine there are many moms just like me, who only want what's best for their kids, who play by the rules (as we learn them) and try to do it right, even if we're not sure what "right" is, only what we think is wrong. There must be other moms who see how much fun their kids are having and just want to keep them in the game, though I wonder how many of them have to tell their sons that they might not be able to pay for next month's lessons, much less the Nike summer camp he is dying to attend.

"He's a nice little player," the blonde woman says. "Not afraid of Jay at all."

My face warms at the compliment. "Well, he probably just doesn't know any better."

"Oh no, he's a fighter, I can tell." The pearls around her neck rattle. "Jay wins so many matches just because those kids get so nervous playing 'a Goldman.' It's good to see someone take it to him."

I look at my pale reflection in her sunglasses and thank her.

"You seem pretty relaxed," she comments. "Some of these parents get more nervous than their kids. Isn't that sick? Just let them play. It's supposed to be fun, and it's not once we get involved." She extends a soft, manicured hand with crimson fingernails. "I'm Anne."

I take her hand and pretend I didn't already know that. We talk like driver and passenger, glancing over occasionally while keeping our eyes on the court. Danny loses a point, drops his racquet, and stares at it with his hands on his hips. Jay takes the ball out of his pocket and hits it over to Danny, who must have just lost the game.

I wonder if Anne knows how much people talk about her family, how the Goldmans represent the bar for tennis in New England. "We're not the Goldmans," people like to say, "but we do our best." Or "We can only spend so much money on tennis, not like the Goldmans." But when families hear that Jay goes to Florida over Christmas for two weeks of training, they send their sons down, too. As long as the Goldmans are around, people will always have something to reach for, as well as an excuse for falling short.

The boys change sides and Jay flips the scorecard. Danny leads, 2-1. Anne leans over and murmurs, "You know, we should get these two together sometime. We're just up the road a bit."

I blush again. "That would be great! I always try to get Danny to make friends with the boys he plays with. All he really knows about Jay is from the rankings." The words repeat in my head as quickly I spoke them.

"Isn't that too bad? Jay really doesn't get to practice with many boys his age because of that. And Martin gets so sick of his little brother pestering him to play. Where are you from?"

"Hartford," I say.

"You poor thing. I'm so glad we can just pop over to the club for these tournaments. So great. Was it a long drive last night?"

"Actually, we came up this morning. I teach a late class on Fridays, and my husband—"

"Oh, Lucy, you really should get here the night before. It's so hard for them to get out of the car after a long ride and have to play. I might sound like a tennis mother right now, but we should at least give them the best chance to play well."

I'd never thought about that. Most of the time I'm just glad we make it in one piece and on time. If I'm feeling especially lucky, I hope we don't leave anything important at home. I don't tell her that we had to rent a car because I didn't trust mine.

"But really Lucy, we would love to have Danny over some time," Anne says. "We can have him picked up, too."

"That's very kind of you."

"Don't mention it. We have *tons* of space and Danny would have so much fun. Jay likes to stay out in the pool house when he has friends over, but we keep a close eye on them. In fact, I have a great idea! Is Danny playing the NNQ next month?"

I nod, trying to remember what NNQ stands for: National-something-or-other-Qualifier.

"Then why don't you send him up Friday and he can spend the night? He can get a good dinner, a good night's sleep, and a real breakfast before his match. And he and Jay can warm up together!"

Anne turns back to the match, smiling pleasantly. I return to my grading with her words echoing in my mind.

Out!

What! Are you sure?

I look up and see Jay walking toward the net. *That wasn't on the line?* he asks.

Danny just shakes his head and holds up his index finger, signaling that the ball was out. Jay takes a long look at where the ball landed and turns around, disgusted. I glance at Anne, who just bounces her shoulders, unaffected.

Danny explained it to me once. Each player is responsible for making calls on balls that land on his side of the court. If his opponent disagrees, he can ask if he's sure, but after that, he must accept the call. If the player isn't sure whether the ball was in or not, he then gives his opponent the benefit of the doubt, and the ball is good. A lot of kids call lets when they're not sure, replaying the point because they don't want to hurt anyone's feelings, but they're not supposed to. It's either in or out, Danny said.

The scorecard reads 5-4, Danny. It's obvious even to me that Jay is by far the best player Danny's ever faced, and also that Danny is playing especially well. Whenever Danny loses, I don't really understand why. He always looks just as good as his opponent, but Chick, a local pro who occasionally coaches Danny free of charge, knowing that the weekly group lessons at the club are all we can afford, tells me he needs to get "match tough." Danny has great ability, Chick says, but doesn't yet know how to use it when winning or losing is at stake. And the only way to get match tough is to play more under pressure. So I go along with Chick and sign Danny up for all the tournaments he can handle, but it makes me a little uneasy. It feels wrong, putting these kids out there on their own at such a young age, not allowing them any coaching and giving only quiet support—subdued clapping, occasional compliments for good shots—and getting dirty looks if we cheer too loud.

I take a break from grading and look at my calendar. "So Anne, what weekend is that NNQ?"

"You should really watch this match," she says, nodding toward the court. "That's the first set that Jay's lost in twelves in a long time."

I double-check the scorecards. "Wow. I guess Danny's playing pretty well."

"You could say that."

"Well, ah, I was just looking at my calendar for next month. I might be able to take Danny up to your place, after all."

Anne gives me a strange look. "You should really watch this match," she repeats, and stares at me an extra second before turning away.

Jay wins the first game of the second set, and they switch sides again. I point to Danny's jug with my eyebrows raised, but he just shakes his head again. I acquiesce and notice Oscar staring at me. I look down and read a paper with animation, feeling as if he caught me doing something I shouldn't.

Out!

Anne flinches and raises her eyebrows at me. I was watching this time. We're sitting right on the baseline extended and that ball was in. Close, but in. I immediately feel a little rotten inside, like having witnessed someone litter or steal a handful of candy from the bulk bins. I try to catch Danny's eye but he's fiddling with his strings and pumping his fist. He's so into the match, I think he might have really thought the ball was out. I shake my head and shrug to Anne. These things usually even out— that's what Chick told me when Danny first started, when I could not believe how many bad calls some boys made. Anyway, Danny usually gives his opponents too many calls, I think. Maybe it's good that he's starting to call them tighter. The ball was still in, and Danny was wrong, but I'm sure he didn't mean it. I bury my head back into my work and wait for the embarrassment to pass.

Danny hits an un-returnable serve and ties the second set at 2-2. He's playing so well right now and I'm so proud of him. Actually being able to see the improvement starts to make it all worth it, the driving to lessons, the constantly worrying about money, the spending weekends at tennis clubs, which is just as well, because my chest gets tight when I'm around Stan these days.

Out!

"Lucy, did you see that?" Anne says.

"Hmm?" I say absently, trying to figure out what to write on this student's essay. "What happened?"

"Please. Don't pretend you didn't see that. I guess those coaches in Hartford haven't told your boy that if a ball lands on the line, it's in. Maybe he just isn't used to playing on a decent court."

I'm stunned. I had not seen the point, and I can't believe what I just heard. So far I've only seen Danny make that one bad call. I decide to give Anne the benefit of the doubt. "I'm sorry, Anne," I say. "I really wasn't watching. Jay's a great player. I'm sure he'll win. Danny's just no match for him."

Out!

Danny calls another close one and Anne gasps loud enough to turn heads on three courts, and makes cute little Mark Powell miss a serve. Mark looks over at Anne and mumbles something. I can read his lips: *fucking bitch.*

"Lucy, this is ridiculous," Anne says. "If your boy's this worried about losing, I can just have Jay default. We don't need this match that badly."

"Danny," I whisper as loud as I can, glancing sideways at the other parents. "Danny!"

Danny finally looks at me. His expression says, You're not supposed to talk to me, Mom.

"I know, honey." I realize I haven't thought about what to say. I finally decide on, "Try to pay attention to your calls, OK?"

He can't hear me. *What?* It comes out very loud. Oscar and the Powers look over at me.

"Honey, be sure about your calls," I say, trying to keep my voice low. "Some of those balls are pretty close." I feel awful saying this, and regret it immediately. Why should Danny have to play under this scrutiny? Doesn't he have enough on his mind? The last thing he needs to think about is his own mother insinuating that he's a cheater. I saw Jay call some close balls out and Danny didn't utter a word.

I look for Oscar and I'm relieved when I don't see him at the desk.

"Excuse me." Oscar appears next to me, peering down with his hands clasped behind his back. "You're not allowed to talk to your son during the match."

"Oh! I'm sorry. I'm just trying to tell him—"

"I don't care. Stop talking to him."

"I—I'm not coaching him," I say. "I was just telling him to be careful about his line calls." I want to show Oscar that we play fair. I quickly explain to him why I was talking to Danny. "Anne, can you help me out here?"

"What?" She acts as if she has just noticed us.

Oscar waits for confirmation from Anne, who crosses her legs and slowly leans forward, pearls dangling in front of her stretched shirt. Oscar's glasses are tinted just lightly enough that I can see his eyes wander down her neckline.

"Oh, Oscar, she wasn't doing anything," Anne says. "Her boy was just trying to get some cheap points and I told her to make him stop. You know how Jay's too nice to say anything. Don't you have better things to do than watch some twelve-year-olds play? I'm sure there are some girls over on court nine who are probably far more interesting to you."

Oscar laughs uncomfortably and fixes on me. "I'll let it go this time, but don't do it again," he says. "I'm tired of parents trying to take advantage of the rules. If I catch you cheating any more, you won't be invited back to this club." He walks over to the fence and stands against it with his arms folded. When the boys change ends, he follows Danny over to his side.

What a pompous bastard, I think. I taste the bile rising in my throat and I hate the way I feel, how quickly my mood has been darkened by Oscar's subtle reminder that Danny and I don't belong here. All the worries that usually stay outside the tennis club begin to leak through, and I wonder if Tom made it to soccer, how long our car will keep running, when Stan will find a job, and if that will solve our problems. Even the air feels a little colder, the wind beginning to blow in from the water.

The boys paid no attention to what was going on and started playing again. Danny is making a lot of close calls, most of them on the baseline or on the far sideline, but he doesn't really seem to notice Oscar. For the first time, I catch myself thinking about what might happen if Danny won, beating the number one player in New England, and with a national ranking, no less. That would mean Danny's good enough to be number one, too. The scorecards read 4-3, Danny.

Then I think, We can't afford this. It was okay when he just played once a week at the city courts, but now he runs through shoes every few months and has changed racquets twice. And the strings! He breaks them almost every a week, twenty dollars each time, not counting the labor the pro shop charges for the job. We started having to buy string in bulk, big three-hundred-foot reels, and Stan finally bought a machine and learned how to string. Now Danny strings for himself. The machine was three hundred dollars, but that's what we would have paid for four months of restringing. Danny has gotten so good so fast, I don't know if we can support him for six more years. And national tournaments? Donna says there are grants and scholarships available, even for younger players like Danny, but I wouldn't even know where to start to look for those.

Everyone says all this will help Danny get into college, maybe even pay for it, but I don't know if we can hold out until then. And I don't see why he can't pay for college without tennis. He got into Kingswood-Oxford without tennis. Now Donna tells me Cheshire Friends just gave a nine-year-old a tennis scholarship, and that I'm naïve when I express my disbelief—that's just how things are, Lucy. You've got to play the game. As much as I want it, we just aren't cut out to be a tennis family. Tennis families have mid-six-figure incomes, a stay-at-home wife, vacation homes. We couldn't even afford to join East Hartford Tennis & Fitness when Stan was still working. But who am I to keep Danny from going where the game can take him?

"Come on, Jay," Anne barks, clapping her hands fast and angrily. I almost say something to encourage Danny, but restrain myself.

Jay looks at his mother with wide eyes after every point.

"Let's go, Jay. Right here," she says.

Danny double faults.

"Yes, Jay!" Anne shouts. "Here we go. Let's take advantage."

As obnoxious as I find it, it seems to work. Jay starts making fewer mistakes, and Danny looks tired, not getting to all of Jay's shots. Jay wins three straight games to go up 6-5 before Danny manages to hold his serve to make it 6-6. Anne relaxes a little once they start the tiebreaker, where the players alternate serves and the first one to win seven points by a margin of two wins the set. The boys play these at their lessons, and the only time Danny has ever beaten Chick was during a tiebreaker.

The college kid waves to Oscar and holds up a phone. He and Oscar have a silent, pantomimed conversation and Oscar brushes him off.

Out!

No way. Jay looks over at his mother and Oscar, furious. Danny called a ball out that was right on the line. *Did you see that?*

I did. But I know Oscar didn't, and I wait for him to make eye contact with me.

"Oscar. That. Ball. Was. Right. On. The. Line." Anne squeezes it out between clenched teeth. "You better overrule that."

Oscar's eyes meet mine and I stare back. He deflates.

"Anne, I didn't see that point," he says. "I can't overrule it."

Anne looks sunburned. "Goddammit, Oscar, that boy's been cheating Jay all . . . *fucking* day," she hisses, "and now he does it again right in front of you! What the hell are you good for?"

Oscar holds up his finger to Jay, then opens his palms apologetically. Jay's shoulders sag and he walks away. According to the rules, it wouldn't have mattered if the entire club had seen Danny make a bad call; Oscar was the only one who could have changed it, although I now wish he *had* seen the point, so he might have relieved me of having to deal with Danny after the match.

Someone must have spread the word that Jay Goldman was losing. Just about everyone who isn't playing has crowded around us, though nobody takes the empty seat next to me. Even the boys playing on the next court wait to see who wins the point before turning back to their own match. The air buzzes with whispers, and I take the papers off my lap—who am I kidding? Groans and gasps punctuate each point, but the crowd doesn't seem to be pulling for Danny so much as they are intrigued by the possibility of seeing Jay lose, if only because it hasn't happened in so long. Danny wins four more points before he finally seems to notice all the attention and gets self-conscious, eyes darting at the people between points. Jay roars back and ties it at 6-all.

The boys trade points and switch sides twice until Danny's ball skids off a line and Jay hits his shot long, obviously long, far enough out that Danny simply catches the ball after it bounces and steps up to serve for the match, up 12-11. Jay makes no argument.

Danny spins in his serve, his grunt making it seem faster than it really is. Jay returns and they moonball it back and forth, standing six feet behind the baseline and lobbing balls with no pace, shots Danny used to hit when he was lugging around racquets as big as he was, making contact—by accident, if you had asked me then—with every fifth ball that Chick baby-tossed to him, but having so much fun and looking so proud and happy when he hit a good one, screaming and jumping so ecstatically I felt bad for taking him home, and he would beg me, just one more, Mommy, please? And Chick would toss him ten more one mores, or however many he had to until Danny hit another and on the way home all he would talk about was how many good balls he hit and I would tell him how proud I was.

Sometimes we stopped by Stan's office at school, where Stan would take him to the dining hall to get something to eat while I caught a quick nap on the old yarn couch, chalk dust rising every time I adjusted my position. Back at the office, Stan and I would curl up together and catch up on our days as Danny took giant, grimacing bites of pizza, sitting on his knees in Stan's chair, spinning around slowly, dreamily, and when finished, climbed off to draw dinosaurs on the dry erase board until it was time for us to go home, together. It seems like Danny got bigger and stronger in an instant, hitting harder, spinning shots and walking around the court like the players he watched on television, scrunching up his face in concentration, slumping his shoulders when he lost a point, smacking his head and pulling his hair, beseeching a missed shot to go in, caring so much.

I realize I'm counting the shots in the rally. After hitting the twenty-fifth ball, Danny runs in to the net. Jay winds up and hits a ball hard and flat and low to Danny's forehand. Danny yelps and lunges for the ball, just barely getting his racquet on it, and it amazingly goes back over. But now he's a sitting duck. Jay scampers up to the short bouncing ball and rips another forehand. Danny dives again and I hear the ball nick the top of his racquet before landing wide of the sideline. Jay's point, because Danny touched the ball. Jay hops and pivots to walk back, making a fist. *Come on!*

With the score tied again, the tension that had built up during the point empties out, and everyone sags. Everyone except for me, that is, because I keep my eyes on Danny, and I am the first to see him jumping up and down, waving his arms. *Yes! Yes, I won!* He stands over the net and holds out his hand. Jay gives him a strange look. *Are you crazy?* I can feel Anne's and everyone else's eyes turn onto me. Jay says that he heard the ball hit Danny's racquet, and Danny shakes his head. *No, I didn't touch it. That ball was out and it's my point, 13-11. I win.* Then I see Anne screaming at me, at Oscar, at everyone who's watching this little son of a bitch try to hook the match from poor Jay, who stayed home from sailing to play in this piece of shit tournament and this is the thanks we get? Danny stands without moving, his arm extended, waiting for the handshake, a distant, calm smile on his face. Jay looks dazed as he walks to the net, instinct and etiquette pushing him toward Danny, putting his fingers into Danny's palm. Danny squeezes them to make it official.

Anne shrieks and runs onto the court. She clamps one hand onto Jay's wrist and takes out her cell phone with the other, using her teeth to pull out the antenna as she stomps over toward the pro shop. Danny throws his gear into his bag and scrambles off the court, almost tripping in excitement. "Mom, can you believe I won?" he squeals.

Normally, we would find a quiet place to eat our packed lunches and Danny would read a book or play Game Boy until it's time for his next match, but I know I ought to say something. I just haven't a clue where to start, especially with all the people who have formed a loose ring around us, watching and whispering to each other. Danny's so proud of himself he can hardly stand still, his cheeks flushed and hair spiked with sweat. I try to smile. "Those were some awfully close calls out there," I say quietly.

Danny's grin wavers and he quickly, too quickly, looks away, suddenly interested in a match still being played. "Yeah," he says. "I guess."

I take a deep breath. "Were you sure about all of them?"

"Huh?"

"Do you think . . . you might have gotten some of them wrong?"

"I don't know."

Danny doesn't say anything more. Every move he makes, like scratching his head or rubbing his nose or shifting his weight onto his left leg, suddenly bears the mark of self-conscious calculation.

"Honey?" I say.

"What?"

"I just wonder if maybe you might have been so caught up in the match that you didn't realize what you were doing." I'm offering Danny an excuse, but he doesn't take it. He just stares at the other courts. "Did you make those calls on purpose?"

"Mom!" His voice gets high and his eyes flicker, as if he's looking for an escape. "I just beat *Jay Goldman.*"

Behind Danny's mask of indignation I can see him trying to figure out what he should say, but all the effort he puts into acting naturally only makes him seem more like someone else's son. I know I should admonish him, tell him what he had done wrong, use this as a moment of teaching. But all I do is wrap my arms around his bony shoulders and hope that the right words will seep into him.

"Sorry, Mom," he says, muffled by my shoulder. "I just wish you were happier about me beating them."

I wonder how long he has been feeling like this, how long he has known about the unfairness of there being an us and a them. The ring of players and parents grows tighter, and as I lift my head to meet their gazes, I think about all the things those people have done to get ahead, and how it seems like so many things in Danny's life, maybe even me, have conspired to leave him behind. After looking into the sun all morning, my face finally begins to cool. I squeeze my son again and we walk over to find out when he plays next.

Eric-Emmanuel Schmitt
The Most Beautiful Book in the World

Translated from French
by Alison Anderson

A shiver of hope went through them when they first saw Olga.

To be sure, she did not seem particularly kind. Tall, dry, with a prominent jaw-bone, jutting elbows, and sallow skin, when she first came in she did not look at a single woman in the ward. She sat down on the wobbly bunk she'd been assigned, put away her belongings at the bottom of the wooden chest, listened to the guard, shouting the rules at her as if the latter were braying Morse code, did not turn her head until she was informed of the location of the washroom and then, once the guard had left, she stretched out on her back, cracked her knuckles, and gave herself over to the contemplation of the blackened planks on the ceiling.

"Have you seen her hair?" murmured Tatyana.

The prisoners did not understand what Tatyana meant by that.

The newcomer had a thick mane of hair—frizzy, robust, coarse, which doubled the volume of her head. Such health and vigor—the sort of thing you usually only saw on the head of an African woman. But Olga, despite her olive skin, did not look remotely African, and must have come from somewhere in the Soviet Union, since here she was now in Siberia, in this women's camp where the regime punished those who did not think in the orthodox fashion.

"What about her hair, then?"

"I think she's from the Caucasus."

"You're right. Their women often have straw-like hair."

"Yes, horrible hair, isn't it."

"Not at all! It's magnificent! With my flat, fine hair, I could only dream of having hair like that."

"I'd rather die. It looks like horsehair."

"No—pubic hair!"

Giggling, quickly stifled, accompanied Lily's last remark.

Tatyana frowned and silenced the group by pointing out: "Her hair might offer us the solution."

Eager to please Tatyana, whom they treated as their leader even though she was just an ordinary prisoner like the others, they tried to concentrate on what they had failed to grasp: how could a stranger's hair offer any solution to the lives they were leading—that of political deviants being forcibly re-educated?

That night a thick snowfall had buried the camp. Outside, everything was dark except for the lantern that the storm was trying to extinguish. The temperature, well below zero, did not help them to concentrate.

"Do you mean . . ."

"Yes. I mean you can hide quite a few things in a head of hair like that."

They observed a moment of respectful silence. One of them finally guessed: "With her she has brought a . . ."

"Yes!"

Lily, a gentle blonde woman who, despite the climate, the rigors of work, and the deplorable food, was still as round as any kept woman, now voiced a certain skepticism.

"Well, she'll have to have thought of it first."

"Why would she not have?"

"Well I certainly wouldn't have thought of it before coming here."

"And I'm referring to her, not to you."

Well aware that Tatyana would always have the final word, Lily refrained from voicing her annoyance, and went back to sewing the hem of her woolen skirt.

They listened to the icy howling of the storm.

Leaving her companions behind, Tatyana went down the row, approached the foot of the newcomer's bed, and stood there for a while, waiting for a sign that would indicate she had been noticed.

A feeble flame was dying in the stove.

After a few minutes, during which she obtained no reaction, Tatyana resolved to break the silence: "What's your name?"

A deep voice answered, "Olga." Her lips had not moved.

"And why are you here?"

No reaction on Olga's face. A mask of wax.

"I expect, like all of us, you were Stalin's preferred fiancée and he got bored with you?"

She thought she was saying something funny, an almost ritual witticism that greeted all the opponents to the Stalinist regime; her words slid over the stranger like a pebble over ice.

"My name's Tatyana. Would you like me to introduce the others?"

"There'll be time enough for that, no?"

"There certainly will . . . we'll be in this hole for months, or years . . . we might even die here."

"So we have time."

To conclude, Olga closed her eyes and turned to face the wall, leaving only her angular shoulders to carry on the conversation.

Realizing she would get nothing more out of her, Tatyana went back to join the others.

"A tough nut. Which is reassuring. There's a chance that . . ."

Nodding approvingly, even Lily, they decided to wait.

In the week that followed, the newcomer offered up no more than a sentence a day, and even that had to be forced out of her. Such behavior seemed to validate the hopes of the oldest prisoners.

"I'm sure she's thought about it," said Lily eventually, more convinced with each passing hour. "She is definitely the type who would think about it."

The day brought little light. The fog forced its grayness upon it, and when it lifted, an impenetrable screen of oppressive clouds weighed upon the camp, like an army of sentinels.

"I expect, like all of us, you were Stalin's preferred fiancée and he got bored with you?"

As no one had been able to inspire Olga's trust, the women counted on the shower to show them whether the newcomer was hiding a . . . But it was so cold that no one attempted, anymore, to get undressed; so impossible would it be to get dry and warm after such an undertaking that everyone resorted to a furtive, minimal scrub. One rainy morning they discovered, moreover, that Olga's mane was so thick that the drops slid over it without adhering; her hair was waterproof.

"Never mind," ventured Tatyana, "we'll have to take the risk."

"Of asking her?"

"No. Of showing her."

"And what if she's a spy? What if she's been sent here to trap us?"

"She's not the type," said Tatyana.

"No, she's not the type at all," confirmed Lily, pulling on a thread in her sewing.

"Yes she is the type! She's playing silent, tough, unfriendly, the sort who won't get close to anyone: isn't that the very best way to make us trust her?"

It was Irina who was vociferating in this manner, surprising the other women, surprising her own self, stupefied by the coherence of her reasoning. Astonished, she went on: "I can just imagine that if someone entrusted me with spying on a hut full of women, there would be no better way to go about it. Pass myself off as the quiet, solitary sort and, over time, gain the others' trust. That's cleverer than acting friendly, no? We may have been infiltrated by the biggest tattletale in the Soviet Union."

Lily was suddenly so convinced of this that she rammed her needle into the thick of her finger. A drop of blood formed, and she looked at it, terrified.

"I want to be moved into another hut, quick!"

Tatyana intervened.

"I understand your reasoning, Irina, but that's all it is, reasoning. As for me, my intuition tells me the opposite. We can trust her, she's like us. Or even harder than we are."

"Let's wait. Because if we are caught . . ."

"Yes, you're right. Let's wait. And above all, let's try to push her to the breaking point. Let's stop talking to her. If she's a spy who's been planted here to inform on us, she'll panic and try to get closer to us. With every step she takes she'll reveal her strategy."

"Good point," confirmed Irina. "Let's ignore her and see how she reacts."

"It's dreadful . . ." sighed Lily, licking her finger to speed the scarring.

For ten days, not one prisoner in Ward 13 said a word to Olga. At first she didn't seem to notice and then, once she was aware of it, her gaze grew harder, almost mineral; and yet she did not make the slightest gesture to break the wall of silence. She accepted her isolation.

After they had had their soup, the women gathered around Tatyana.

"There's our proof, no? She didn't crack."

"Yes, it's terrifying."

"Oh, Lily, everything terrifies you."

"You have to admit it's a nightmare: to be rejected by the group, then realize, and not lift a finger to prevent such exclusion! It's hardly human . . . I wonder if that Olga has a heart."

"Who's to say she isn't suffering?"

Lily put down her sewing, her needle stuck through the thick fold of cloth; she hadn't thought of this. Her eyes immediately filled with tears.

"Have we made her unhappy?"

"I think she was unhappy when she got here and she's even unhappier now."

"Poor woman! And it's our fault . . ."

"I think, above all, that we can count on her."

"Yes, you're right," exclaimed Lily, drying her tears with her sleeve. "Let's confide in her now, quickly. It hurts me too much to think that she's just a prisoner like the rest of us and we're making her troubles worse by making life impossible for her."

After a few minutes of consultation, the women decided they would risk unveiling their plan, and Tatyana would take the initiative.

After that, the camp lapsed again into its drowsiness; outside, the frost was extreme; a few furtive squirrels scrabbled across the snow among the huts.

With her left hand Olga was crumbling an old crust of bread; with the other she was holding her empty dish.

Tatyana came over.

"Did you know that you're allowed a pack of cigarettes every two days?"

"Has it occurred to you that I have noticed and that I've been smoking?"

Olga's words had sprung from her mouth sharply, precipitously; the sudden cessation of a week of silence accelerated her elocution.

Tatyana noticed that despite her aggressive tone, Olga had spoken more than usual. She must be missing human contact . . . so Tatyana reckoned it was all right to continue.

"Since you notice everything, you will have seen no doubt that none of us smokes. Or that we only smoke now and again when the guards are around."

"Uh . . . yes. No. What do you mean?"

"Haven't you wondered what we use our cigarettes for?"

"Oh, I see; you swap them. You use them for cash in the camp. You want to sell me some? I don't have anything to pay with . . ."

"You're mistaken."

"So if you don't pay with money, what do you pay with?"

Olga looked at Tatyana with a suspicious scowl, as if she knew ahead of time that whatever she was about to discover would disgust her. So Tatyana took her time to reply: "We don't sell our cigarettes, we don't swap them either. We use them for something other than smoking."

Because she sensed she had piqued Olga's curiosity, Tatyana broke off the discussion, well aware that she would have a stronger case if the other woman had to come back to her to find out the rest.

That very evening, Olga went over to Tatyana and looked at her for a long time, as if to ask her to break the silence. In vain. Tatyana repaid her in kind for the first evening.

Olga eventually capitulated: "Right, what do you do with the cigarettes?"

Tatyana turned to her with a searching look.

"Did you leave people you love behind?"

Olga's only reply was a fleeting, pained expression.

"So did we," continued Tatyana, "we miss our men, but why should we be more worried for their sake than for our own? They're in another camp. No, what really hurts, is the children . . ."

Tatyana's voice faltered: the image of her two daughters had just pricked her conscience. Out of compassion, Olga placed her hand on Tatyana's shoulder: a sturdy, powerful hand, not unlike a man's.

"I understand, Tatyana. I have also left a daughter behind. Fortunately, she's twenty-one."

"My girls are eight and ten . . ."

It took all her remaining strength to keep from crying. Besides, what more was there to add?

Brusquely, Olga pulled Tatyana against her shoulder and Tatyana—tough Tatyana, the network leader, the eternal rebel—because she had found someone tougher than herself, wept for a moment against a stranger's chest.

Safely unburdened of her surfeit emotion, she picked up the thread of her thoughts.

"This is what we use the cigarettes for: we empty out the tobacco, and we keep the papers. Afterwards, by gluing the papers together, we can make a real sheet of paper. Here, come with me, I'll show you."

Tatyana lifted up a floor board and from a hiding place full of potatoes she removed a crackling pile of cigarette papers, where each joint, each glued crease thickened the delicate tissues, as if they were some millennial papyrus discovered in Siberia through some aberration of archeology.

She placed the sheets carefully on Olga's knees.

"There. One of us is bound to get out of here someday . . . and she'll take our messages with her."

"Fine."

"But you may have noticed, there's a problem."

"Yes, I can see that the pages are blank."

"Yes, blank on both sides. Because we don't have a pen or ink. I tried to write with my own blood, I stole a pin from Lily, but it fades too quickly . . . And besides, I don't scar well. Something to do with my platelets. Malnutrition. I don't want to go to the infirmary, it might make them suspicious."

"Why are you telling me this? What does it have to do with me?"

"Well, I suppose that you too would like to write to your daughter?"

Olga allows a full minute of thickening silence to go by then says, gruffly, "Yes."

"So here's what we'll do: we'll provide you with the paper, and you get us the pencil."

"Now why would you think I have a pencil? That's the first thing they take off us when they arrest us. And we were all searched several times over before coming here."

"Your hair . . ."

Tatyana pointed to the thick halo of hair surrounding Olga's stern face. And went on staring at her.

"When I first saw you, I thought that . . ."

Olga interrupted her with her hand and, for the first time, she smiled.

"You are correct."

As Tatyana's eyes filled with wonder, Olga slipped her hand behind her ear, dug about in her curls and then, her eyes shining, she pulled out a narrow pencil and handed it to her fellow prisoner.

"It's a deal."

It is no easy thing to measure the joy that warmed the women's hearts during the days which followed. Through that little pencil lead they had once again found their hearts, their ties with the world from before, a way to embrace their children.

Captivity no longer seemed as arduous. Nor did guilt. For some of them did feel terrible remorse for the fact that they had put their political activities before their family life; now that they had been shipped off to the depths of the gulag, leaving their children at the mercy of a society they had despised and fought against, they could not help but regret their militancy and suspect that they had failed in their duty, and thus proven themselves to be bad mothers. Would it not have been better to simply keep quiet, like so many other Soviet women, and immerse themselves in domestic values? To save their own skins, and the skins of their loved ones, rather than to struggle to save everyone's?

While each of the prisoners had several sheets of paper, there was only one pencil. So after several meetings they agreed that each woman would have the right to three full sheets before all of them were bound together in a stitched notebook which would be smuggled out at the first opportunity.

The second rule: each woman must write her pages without making any mistakes, in order not to waste the pencil lead.

While their decision was greeted with general enthusiasm that evening, the days that followed were more troublesome. Confronted with the obligation to concentrate all their thoughts onto three small sheets, each woman struggled: how to put together three essential pages, three testamentary pages that would imprint the essence of a life, that would pass on to their children their souls and their values, and convey for all eternity the significance of their time on earth?

The undertaking became a torture. Every evening sobs could be heard from the bunks. Some of the women lost sleep over it; others moaned in their dreams.

The moment they could seize a break in their forced labor, they would try to exchange their ideas.

"I'm going to tell my daughter why I am here and not with her. So that she'll understand, and maybe she'll forgive me."

"Three pages of guilty conscience to give yourself a clear conscience—do you really think that's a good idea?"

"I want to tell my daughter how I met her father, so that she'll know that she was born because of the love between us."

"Oh yes? And what if all she really cares about is finding out why you didn't stick around to love her."

"I want to tell my three daughters about their birth, because each of their births was the most beautiful moment in my life."

"That's a bit short, no? You don't think they'll be sorry you restricted your memories to their arrival on the scene? You'd do better to talk about what came afterwards."

"I want to tell them what I would like to do for them."

"Hmm."

In the course of their discussions, they uncovered a singular detail: all of them had given birth to daughters. The coincidence amused them, then surprised them, to such a degree that they came to wonder whether the decision to incarcerate all the mothers of daughters together in Ward 13 had not been deliberate on the part of the authorities.

But this diversion did not bring an end to their ordeal: what should they write?

Every evening Olga would wave the pencil and call out, "Who wants to begin?"

Every evening a diffuse silence would settle over the women. Time passed, perceptibly, like stalactites dripping from the ceiling of a cave. The women, heads down, waited for one of them to shout, "Me!" and to deliver them temporarily from their troubles but, after a few coughs and furtive glances, the most courageous would eventually say that they were still thinking.

"I've nearly got it . . . tomorrow perhaps."

"Yes, me too, I'm getting there, but I'm not quite sure . . ."

The days went by, whirling with snow flurries, crisp with immaculate frost. Although the prisoners had waited two years for the pencil, three months had already gone by and not one of them asked for the pencil or even accepted it.

So imagine their surprise when one Sunday, after Olga had lifted up the object and uttered the ritual words, Lily answered eagerly, "I'll have it, thanks."

They turned around, stunned, to look at plump, blonde Lily, the most scatterbrained of them all, the most sentimental, the least headstrong—in short: the most normal. If someone had tried to forecast who among the prisoners would be first to start writing her three pages, Lily would surely have been placed among the stragglers. First would be Tatyana, or perhaps Olga, or even Irina—but sweet, ordinary Lily?

Tatyana could not help but stammer, "Lily . . . are you sure?"

"Yes, I think so."

"You're not going to . . . scribble, make a mistake . . . well, wear down the pencil?"

"No, I've had a good think: I'll manage without any mistakes."

Skeptical, Olga handed Lily the pencil. As she was giving it to her, she exchanged glances with Tatyana, who seemed to confirm that they were surelye committing a blunder.

On the days that followed, the women in Ward 13 stared at Lily every time she would go off on her own to write, sitting on the floor, alternating inspiration—eyes raised to the ceiling—and expiration, her shoulders curved to hide the marks she was making on the paper from the others.

On Wednesday she announced, satisfied, "I've finished. Who wants the pencil?"

A gloomy silence met her question.

"Who wants the pencil?"

Not a single woman dared look at another. Lily concluded, calmly, "Right, then I'll put it back in Olga's hair until tomorrow."

Olga merely grunted when Lily hid the object deep in her curls.

Anyone other than Lily—not as good, more aware of the complexities of the human heart—might have noticed that the women in the ward were now training jealous gazes upon her, perhaps even a bit of hatred. How had Lily, who really was close to being a moron, managed to succeed where the others had failed?

A week went by, and every evening was another opportunity for the women to relive their defeat.

Finally, the following Wednesday at midnight, when the sound of breathing indicated that most of the women were fast asleep, Tatyana, tired of tossing and turning in her bunk, dragged herself silently over to Lily's bunk.

Lily smiled at her, gazing up at the dark ceiling.

"Lily, I beg you, can you tell me what you wrote?"

"Of course, Tatyana, would you like to read it?"

"Yes."

How would she manage? It was after curfew.

Tatyana huddled at the window. Beyond a spider's web was a field of pure snow, made blue by moonlight; if she twisted her neck, Tatyana could just make out the three small pages.

Lily drew near and asked, her tone that of a little girl who has done something naughty, "Well, what do you think?"

"Lily, you're a genius."

And Tatyana took Lily in her arms to kiss her several times over on her plump cheeks.

The next morning Tatyana asked two favors of Lily: permission to follow her example, and permission to share it with the other women.

Lily lowered her lashes, blushed as if she'd just been offered a bouquet of flowers, and chirped a few words which—though garbled, a sort of cooing in her throat—meant yes.

EPILOGUE
Moscow, December 2005.

Fifty years have passed since these events took place.

The man who is writing these lines is visiting Russia. The Soviet regime has fallen, and there are no more camps—although this in no way means that injustice is a thing of the past.

In the salons of the embassy of France I meet the artists who for years now have been putting on my plays.

Among them is a woman in her sixties who seizes my arm with a sort of affectionate familiarity, a mixture of brazenness and respect. Her smile glows with kindness. It is impossible to resist the mauve of her eyes . . . I follow her over to the window of the palace, with its view over the lights of Moscow.

"Would you like me to show you the most beautiful book in the world?"

"And here I was clinging to hopes I'd written it myself, and you tell me I'm too late. What a blow! Are you sure of this? The most beautiful book in the world?"

"Yes. Other people might write beautiful books, but this one is the most beautiful."

We sit down on one of those oversized, worn sofas that must adorn the grand salons of embassies the world over.

She tells me about her mother, Lily, who spent several years in the gulag, and then about the women who shared that time with her, and finally the story of the book, just as I have related it above.

"I'm the one who owns the notebook. Because my mother was the first one to leave ward 13, she managed to sneak it out, sewn in her skirts. Mother has died, the others too. However, the daughters of the imprisoned comrades come to look at it from time to time: we have tea together and talk about our mothers, and then we read through it again. They've entrusted me with the task of looking after it. When I won't be here anymore, I don't know where it will go. Will a museum to take it? I wonder. And yet it is the most beautiful book in the world. The book of our mothers."

She positions her face beneath my own, as if she were going to kiss me, and winks at me.

"Would you like to see it?"

We make an appointment.

The next day, I climb the enormous stairway leading to the apartment she shares with her sister and two cousins.

In the middle of the table, amidst the tea and the sugar cookies, the book is waiting, a notebook of fragile sheets which the decades have left more brittle than ever.

My hostesses settle me into a worn armchair, and I begin to read the most beautiful book in the world, written by those who fought for freedom, rebels whom Stalin considered dangerous, the resistance fighters of ward 13, each of whom had written three sheets to her daughter, fearful that she might never see her again.

On every page there was a recipe.

Rubén Darío
Leopoldo Lugones
Delmira Agustini
Pablo Neruda
Juan Gelman
Alberto Blanco
Six Poets from Latin America

Translated by Ilan Stavans

NOTA BENE

All poets write in a foreign language. The translator's
responsibility is to leave that foreignness intact in another
tongue. Just as a poem, any poem, always asks the reader
to be aware that words and the world are incompatible
realms, the translator must invariably remind the reader
at all times that loss is what words are about everywhere.
The universality of that loss is what makes us human.
It is our fate.   —I.S.

Rubén Darío
Lo fatal

TO RENÉ PÉREZ

The tree is happy for it is barely sentient,
and all the more the hard rock for it feels nothing.
There's no greater pain than being alive,
no bigger despair that conscious life.

To be and not to know, to be without a path,
the dread of having been and a terror to come . . .
The sure freight of being dead tomorrow,
to suffer for life, through darkness, and for

that which we know not and barely suspect,
the tempting flesh, its grape bunch to come,
the tomb that awaits with funeral sprays,
not to know where we go,
nor where we came from . . . !

Leopoldo Lugones
History of My Death

I dreamed of death and it was quite simple:
a silk thread enwrapped me,
and each kiss of yours
tightened me less with every twist.
And each of your kisses
was a day;
and the time between two kisses
a night. Death is quite simple.
And little by little the fatal thread
unwrapped itself. I no longer controlled it
but for a single bit in between my fingers . . .
Then, suddenly, you became cold,
and no longer kissed me . . .
I let the thread go, and my life vanished.

Delmira Agustini
Fiera de amor

Beast of love, I suffer hunger for hearts.
Of pigeons, vultures, roe deer, or lions,
There is no more tempting prey, no more gratifying tastes,
It already strangulated my claws and instinct,
When erected in an almost ethereal plinth,
I was fascinated by a statue of antique emperor.

And I grew in enthusiasm; through the stone stem
My desire ascended like fulminous ivy,
Up to the chest, seemingly nurtured in snow;
And I clamored to the impossible heart . . . the statue,
A custodian of its glory, pure and serene,
With its forehead in Tomorrow and its feet in Yesterday.

My perennial desire, the stone stem
Has been suspended like bloody ivy;
And since then I bite my heart while dreaming
Of the statue, supreme prisoner of my beautiful claw;
It is neither flesh nor marble; a star paste
Bloodless, with neither warmth nor palpitation . . .

With the essence of a superhuman passion!

Pablo Neruda
The Son

Translated by Ilan Stavans with Alison Sparks

Ah son, do you know, do you know
where you come from?

From a lake with seagulls
white and hungry.

Near the winter water
she and I raised
a red bonfire
wearing out our lips
from kissing the soul,
casting all into the fire
burning our lives.

That's how you came to the world.

But she, to see me
and to see you, one day
crossed the oceans,
and I, to hold
her small waist,

wandered all the earth,
across wars and mountains,
through sand and thorns.

That's how you came to the world.

You come from so many places,
from water and earth,
from fire and snow,
you walk from far away
toward us two,
from the terrible love
that has bewitched us,
so we want to know
what you're like, what you say to us,
because you know more
of the world we gave you.

Like a great storm
we shake
the tree of life

to its most hidden
root fibers
and you appear now
singing in the foliage,
in the highest branch
we reach with you.

Juan Gelman
Dibaxu: I

Translated from Ladino

the tremor in my lips/
I mean: the tremor of my kisses
will be heard in your past
with me in your wine/

opening the door of time/
your dream
allows sleeping rain to fall/
give me your rain/

I will stop you/ still
in your rain of sleep/
far inside the thinking/
without fear/ without forgetfulness/

in the house of time
is the past/
under your foot/
dancing/

Dibaxu: XII

what you gave me
is the trembling word
in the hand of time
open for drinking/

silent
the house is
where we kissed
inside the sun/

Alberto Blanco
My Tribe

The earth is the same
    the heavens are different.
The heavens are the same
    the earth is different.

From lake to lake,
from one forest to another:
which is my tribe?
—I ask—
which is my place?

Perhaps I belong to the tribe
of those with no tribe;
or to the tribe of black sheep;
or to a tribe whose ancestors
    come from the future:
a tribe yet to come.

But if I am to belong to a tribe
—I tell myself—
let it be a large tribe,

a strong tribe,
a tribe where nothing and no one
is left outside,
where everyone,
everything and always
have a holy place.

I don't mean a human tribe.
I don't mean a planetary tribe.
I don't even mean a universal tribe.
I mean a tribe about which one cannot speak.

I mean a tribe that forever lived
but whose existence is yet to be proven.

A tribe that has never lived
but whose existence
might now be proven.

Maps

Let's start at the beginning:
Earth is not the earth:
The map is not the territory.
The territory is not the map.

A map is an image.
A map is a way of speaking.
A map is a collection of memories.
A map is a proportional representation.

The four winds, the four rivers, the four doors, the four pillars of the earth of which myths talk about are nothing but the four corners of a map.

Every map is an image, a painting, a metaphor, a description . . .
But not every description, metaphor, image, or, given the case, not every painting is—by necessity—a map.
Although it can become one.

II

A map is nothing—as the Nabi painter Maurice Denis said of all paintings—but an arrangement of forms and colors over a bi-dimensional surface.

If a territory were homogenous, only the profile of the limits of the territory would be accounted in a map.

No trees grow in a map.

A map of the real world is no less imaginary than a map of an imaginary world.

III

A map is nothing but a bi-dimensional representation of a tri-dimensional world visited by a ghost: time.

If we have been able to map a three-dimensional world in two dimensions, it ought to be possible to map a four-dimensional world in three dimensions.

With a holographic map time should be able to be mapped.

Just like the earth does not stop changing with time, the history of maps does not stop changing with history.
Our idea of space changes according to the changes of our idea of time.

IV

Every map begins with a journey.
But, does every journey start with a map?

The map is to a journey what myth is to language.

At the beginning, maps were travel stories.
Later maps were sights at the edge of the horizon: visual narratives.
Finally, seen from a bird's eye: geographical poems.

A map is an artistic manifestation of the fear of the unknown.

V

To look at the earth from above: arrogance of a fake god.

At the beginning the maps of the earth were accompanied by the maps of heaven.
Later on maps were left without a heaven.
If things go on like this, very soon maps will be left without an earth.

Any truth that can be told is no truth.
Words are not what they designate.
Maps of the earth are not the earth.
The stellar charts are not the heavens.

A dot is a town.
A line is a freeway.
A colored surface is a country.
A volume must be the map of a history.

VI

Exterior maps: Geography.
Interior maps: Psychology.
The doors are the senses.
The limits are the body.

The moral to be drawn from the maps has to do with the idea of control, or—in the best of cases—with an idea of conservation.

As one thinks of the direct relation that exists between maps, the earnings, the wars of conquest and the control of time, one cannot but think of the poem's title: "A Chronometer and Artillery Map."

A map the size of a man's ambition.
A man's ambition the size of a referential system.

All points of reference in a map look outward.

VII

Maps are ideal portraits of our mother.

Maps look at us face to face when they showcase their surfaces.
When they want to account for their depth, they look at us sideways.

At the beginning of cartography it was not possible—perhaps not even desirable—to
separate the territories of wakefulness from the landscapes of dream.

What are the colors on a map if not a dream?
The anesthetized memory of our childhood.
The open windows in the cartographer's office.
A fountain of the purest, simplest happiness.

VIII

Every map is an island.

What once was a savage territory is now a map.

All writing is fragmentary.
Every map is fragmentary.

On maps no travel ever takes place.
In poetry there's nothing written.

J.R. Angelella
In Memoriam

1.

I was in a hardware store when my mother text-messaged me: *Dad die2d*.

I got on line to buy a bolt cutter. I called her and said, "Is this another joke?"

She said, "My greatest failure in life is how I raised you."

"What does that say about me?" I asked, and slid cash across the counter.

"I see him in you," she said. "Like a figure in a wax museum."

The counter boy put my bolt cutter in a paper bag. He wore an apron.

"Who you are has everything to do with what I did," she said.

"As a mother?" I asked.

"And a wife," she said.

The counter boy said, "Do you want your change, sir?"

My mother said one more thing and so did I.

2.

I walked west on Fourteenth Street, bolt cutter in hand.

The day was bright. A blue sky pushed down the buildings. A construction crew leaned against some scaffolding, drinking coffee. On the corner, a payphone, tagged with juvenilia.

I knocked the paper bag off the bolt cutter, slapping at the sides.

I tipped the phone off the cradle. It fell and snapped back like a noose and a neck. The bolt cutter severed the hardwired spine of the phone. The phone in my hand, I whipped the spine in circles over my head like the blade of a helicopter.

"The fuck you doing?" a construction worker asked.

"This is no way to get attention, son," another construction worker said.

"My father used to make collect calls to save a buck," I said.

"You're wrong up here," a third construction worker said, tapping her temple.

"This is me mourning," I said and ran against traffic on Fourteenth to Sixth Avenue. I worked my way north, bolt cutter in one hand, phone with the whirligig spine in the other.

3.

On East Fifty-Six and Sixth, I severed four more, stuffing the phones into my pockets, silver spines spiraling out. I approached another and held the phone.

"I'm an artist waiting tables," she said. "I'm always stuck in some stage of grief."

A sidewalk waitress poured coffee for patrons sitting under umbrellas.

"If you have to make a call," she said, holding a cell phone the size of a water bug, "you can use mine."

"Do I look like I need help making a call?" I asked.

"Looks like you haven't had much success," she said.

"This is not a joke," I said, shaking my bolt cutter.

"And those?" she asked, pointing at the phones and spines poking out from my pockets.

"Why do you care?" I asked.

"I'm an artist waiting tables," she said. "I'm always stuck in some stage of grief."

I snapped another spine.

4.

At the Engineers' Gate entrance to Central Park, a clown asked me to donate a dollar to a children's charity. He thumped a tub of coins with his thumb.

"Sorry," I said. "My father died."

"Would you like to donate in his name?" the clown asked.

"He would want me to honk your nose," I said, pinching air between my fingers. "He loved the circus."

"I'm a father too," he said. "It's hardest on the mothers. They can never give what the father inherently knows." He clicked the heels of his over-sized shoes.

"My mother hates the circus," I said.

"My wife does too," he said. "She looks at me different when I'm dressed like this."

"Do you feel different?" I asked.

"I'm almost a lawyer," he said, pulling at his polka-dot lapel. "Or a pro at failing the bar. Depends on how you look at it."

"You want me to donate in his name?" I asked.

"*He* wants you to," he said, squirting water at a businessman from a fake plastic flower.

"I can give you buckets," I said.

"Of what?" he asked.

"See," I said, and pressed the lower beak of the bolt cutter into the keyhole of the payphone and twisted. Coins poured onto the sidewalk. "Buckets."

5.

As I left the hardware store, my mother said one more thing and so did I.

She said, "I need to tell you something I never told your father."

I said, "Never."

Nina Berberova
The Moon

Translated from Russian
by J. Kates

At night the moon wanted to speak out
On the sundial, but could not.
It tried and tried
It tried in every way it knew
To express what was in its mind
In its great silvery brain,
But in vain:
The arrow never left its course,
Shadow did not fall.

And the garden, rooted in place, waited and watched,
And the flowers looked with horror
On this torment.
And afterwards—for millions of years—
The moon made no effort at all to express itself.

Ian W. Douglas
Dark Was the Night

I'm thinking, thinking,
thinking again about starting over,
about this wall in front of me,
how I didn't even see it coming
until it flattened me, until it
laid me out. How it just squats there.
At first I couldn't understand,
I wore my feet out fuming
in its shadow, I cursed and cried and spit
until my face grew lean, my teeth
loose, eyes yellow. How I
carried on: beating the kettle of my empty chest,
leaping feral foot to foot,
howling like a moon-drunk cat.
I stripped, I threw myself down, ate dirt.
I crawled back to my feet and did it again.
Oh how I suffered, how I loved it—
I even prayed.

Postscript to an Argument

Here, in this impossible landscape
lacerated by an implacable wind,
emptiness
                  is not the absence of things
but the emaciated air that somehow sustains
life or the possibility of.

Here, we must live modestly, low
to the ground, humbled, scrub
before the impenetrable
granite faces
—half obscured by ice and cloud—
obstinate in their chill elevations.

Here, we must come to accept
this impoverished soil; the unmitigated
blaze of afternoon;
the raw
unblemished expanse of winter; and that
dull dark unfathomable night.

Life, at these altitudes, is scarce,
unyielding and terrible.
Sex, here,
unutterably mean and precious.

Weather-Man

Wind. And the rain that felled the sky,
lashed from dawn to dusk, blue-faced,
fierce as a child.

"Every season ends in mud." Yes,
though even the smallest things somehow get by.

"Every season ends in mud."
But storms pass. The moon will rise. The stars
one by one take up their battered typewriters.

As in the pastures, beyond the iron gates,
globe thistles nod rain-heavy crowns against
an altered landscape.

Quiet now. Somehow on fire.

Erica McAlpine
To Leuconoë

—AFTER HORACE, ODES 1.11

You should not ask
the gods what end
they've given you and me,
for it is wrong to know.

Nor should you ask
the stars. Better
to take things as they come,
whether there are many winters

left, or if this one
is the last, which just now
pounds the sea
on giant cliffs of stone.

If you are wise,
strain your wines and cut
short far-reaching hopes.
Life is brief—

as I speak the seconds go—
hold on to
day, think little
of tomorrow.

To Pyrrha

—AFTER HORACE, ODES 1.5

What slender youth,
doused in liquid perfumes,
brings you flowers
beneath this gentle cave?

For whom do you tease
your hair back
in two, simple
yellow roses?

How soon shall he
mourn his love,
and mourn the gods
ever-changing, wondering

unaccustomed, at swirling
waves and dark winds?
For he believes you
are golden and untaken—

believes you
will always be loving.
Who cannot feel the falseness
of this breeze?

As for me,
I've put my tablet
on the temple wall,
hung my dripping

garments there,
and prayed and wept
before the almighty god
of the sea.

To the Lyre

—AFTER HORACE, ODES 1.32

My prayer: if ever in sweet idleness
and cool shade I plucked from you a song
lasting one year or many,
then let us now sing,

for you were tuned long ago in Greece
by a warrior heavy with battle and arms,
who steered his battered ship to shore
and all the while sang

of muses, appetite and wine,
of a boy forever clinging to his love,
of Lycus, his deep black eyes
and blacker hair.

Tortoise shell whose strings Apollo
played at Jupiter's feasts, my balm,
my end to endless toil, let us play again—
now's the only time for song.

A Dedication

—AFTER HORACE, ODES 3.22

Guardian of these mountains, of these groves,
maiden goddess of all laboring girls,
Diana, who, called three times,
keeps death away while tri-formed,

this is your pine that hangs above
my roof, tree to which gladly
each year I'll give a boar
just now practicing sidelong thrusts.

Nickolay Todorov
The Dreams of Savages

From daybreak it was clear the world had woken up in a bad mood. The sun threw heat at the frozen earth but only squandered its effort. And when the Arizona desert has trouble being what it is—roasted and shimmering with doom—odds are the day is bound to be a struggle. Cyril Divakov sucked in the dry air, picked up the aluminum mug from the dust and studied the coffee grounds smeared over its walls. All night he had been tormented by an anxiety to read his fortune.

"I see a blazing sun, hot like a toaster oven," he announced, "and a road that leads to the middle of nowhere and evaporates into thin air."

"It is where we go?" asked Ludovic Guily, Cyril Divakov's sole companion, with concern. His French accent hung in the air like a powerful smell.

Cyril Divakov shook his head and offered the words of his grandmother, a gypsy who had once been married to a eunuch. "A road that ends before its time can only indicate a new beginning."

He was a button of a man with a head topped by a cloud of black curls. Five days of crossing the desert had turned his pasty face into brown leather but it didn't matter— the purpose of a great mission fueled him even in his current risky situation.

He urinated over the fire and kicked sand on top to smother it. The blood hounds from Border Patrol could spot one's lost memories from nine mountains away, not to mention a column of cactus ash smoking into the crisp sky. Mexico was forty miles behind and a barren mountain loomed ahead. To the naked eye it was yellow rock parched by a vicious sun—but the topographic map suggested deep canyons slashed by flash floods. Thin snow covered the highest peaks.

"These are the Cimarron Mountains," he said. "After them it's downhill to the freeway. Ten hours by bus and we're on the Santa Monica pier."

Tears of exhaustion welled up in Guily's eyes.

"I know, brother," Cyril Divakov said. "I'll carry the tent."

From day one, Guily had refused to carry anything except an old guitar, which he used for picking French songs of love and yearning. "I am not a fanatic like you," Guily liked to say. "You can force your body to go when it refuses."

They lumbered up the mountain in steep switchbacks, and new blisters cooked Cyril Divakov's feet. The sun squeezed the air and gave him a migraine that drew vomit. His backpack was forty pounds overweight with food and clothes for both of them, but it would be capricious of him to complain—to be able to wander across the American Southwest was already a miracle. Three years before, he had been deported from the country after a decade of pushing a phony asylum application through the loopholes of the immigration system. Disaster had arrived just as he was about to earn his doctorate in astrophysics from that unrivaled factory for geniuses: the California Institute of Technology. A week before defending his dissertation—a complex design to deploy giant mirrors across the universe that would let us look into the past—two INS officers interrupted his lunch in the university cafeteria and escorted him to the airport in handcuffs.

There was nothing that waited for him in the old country except a vacant house and the disgrace of coming back with empty hands. Home was as he remembered it: poverty, envy and corruption; a place where lofty minds were left to rot. It took him less than a day to escape the country again. For the next three years he broke his back in menial jobs in twenty-four countries and five continents and starved to save each penny. He rode buses, trains, ships and a submarine on his meandering journey back to California. In Mexico City he encountered Ludovic Guily, a vagrant living on a floating island in the canals of Xochimilco. The two men shared Guily's jar of mescal and Cyril Divakov's stories about the clashes of galaxies and the vagueness of time. Guily did not believe a single word but still decided to tag along: he had recognized Cyril Divakov as one of those unrelenting idealists who shot at the moon until it fell at their feet, warm and smelling of gunpowder.

That night was a lifetime away as they fought up the blasted rocks of the Cimarron Mountains.

"I read in the newspaper," Guily gulped for air, "that you can live in America for thirty years and they can still kick you out." His face was red and he looked ready to faint.

A wave of righteous indignation rose within Cyril Divakov. "You've only heard the nice stories then," he said. "They deport single mothers and split them from their babies, and send the babies to orphanages. Not to mention the border-crossers . . . nobody knows what happens to them after they're thrown into the detention centers."

It was a depressing topic, better left to die.

They crested the front range of the mountain and on the top the wind whipped their faces. A deep canyon opened before them, chiseled by a creek that was dry in the winter. Cyril Divakov kept the route close to the top, looking down into a thousand feet of naked slope. Saguaro cacti the size of palms covered the canyon walls. In the upper elevations they wore snowcaps that even the mid-day sun could not melt. Caves gaped on the rocks and turkey vultures circled the sky. Cyril Divakov smiled at them; he knew the mind of a scavenger.

"Merde!" a shriek shattered the quiet.

Guily stood with a leg frozen in midair as a diamondback rattled before him with an erect tail and a hissing tongue.

"Did it bite you?" Cyril Divakov shouted.

"I don't know!"

The coffee Cyril Divakov had consumed surged back into his throat. He grabbed a rock and flung it at the snake.

"Don't make it mad!" Guily cried.

The reptile slid away but crept back. Cyril Divakov threw his foot in its direction and felt contact. In moments like these the adrenaline in his veins was more potent than a donkey's kick. He grabbed the rattler's head and glared into its eyes. What would happen if you bit him!, he wanted to scream, and was choked with wrath. He spat at the snake and his lips touched the cold tongue. Who knows what else he might have done if an awareness of the useless rage inside him hadn't opened his mind to reason. He threw the rattler into the brush.

"What are you doing!" Guily screamed. "Kill it!"

"Keep track of your feet, brother!" Cyril Divakov said. "I can't be tying your shoes at every step!"

He sensed an aftershock of guilt, and with good reason: snapping at his partner was a prodigal way to challenge fate; even a weak man is not always useless. Where would Cyril Divakov be without the refill of hope that Guily's songs brought each night? He apologized, but by then the chin of the Frenchman was quivering. He blinked a few times to clear his eyes. "I suppose I've been more of a burden than you expected."

"Nonsense!" Cyril Divakov said. "You've kept me from losing my mind."

The chill of the snake's tongue lingered on his lips and he threw up. As he was burying the vomit with dirt, a flurry of snow pinched his skin. Within a minute a blizzard descended with snowflakes thick and white like grated feta cheese. The wind attacked the two men in spurts, threatening to blow them over, then vanished to leave silence and the smell of dust.

"Who in hell has heard of snow in the desert!" Guily cried.

"It happens every winter."

There are times when life can ambush a man with arctic cold and enough doubts to muddy the faith of a pope. As Cyril Divakov waited out the storm inside the tent, wrapped in a sleeping bag and holding a glove over his nose, he was overtaken by melancholy. Freezing in the desert, evicted from civilization, molested by snakes and fleeing the Border Patrol—such moments of despair corrupted the noble and academic pursuit of science he had once envisioned.

"You are my son and I'm the first one to know that you will be immortal," his mother had told him before he first left for America. A phone call six years later had brought him the news of her death. She had perished alone, corroded by illness and exiled in a house haunted by the ghost of her only son. He missed the funeral because the lie he had devised to stay in the United States kept him locked in the country until his case was reviewed. His mother was buried by neighbors and, four years later, Cyril Divakov was deported anyway. She would sink in shame now if she knew that all he could attain in return for abandoning her was a slab of muck to perch his tent on.

He caught himself escaping into sleep, so he cut his thumb with a pocketknife and poured salt over the wound to sharpen the pain. "The white death will take us if we fall asleep," he explained. His grandfather had used the same trick to prevent himself from dozing off during the guerilla wars. Guily observed with fear and excitement, as if he were standing beside a wild animal.

They did not speak until the afternoon. The wind howled with a thousand voices in the unreachable caves above. When it became clear that the white confusion outside was only gaining force, Cyril Divakov urinated on his cut finger to disinfect the wound.

"We'll go to the bottom of the canyon," he said.

They scrambled down the precipitous grade, pushed by the weight of their backpacks, digging their heels to stop the slide and starting avalanches of dirt. Cyril Divakov fell many times and impaled his hand on a cactus. It caused him much pain but there was nothing he could do.

By the time they reached the bottom they were covered in brown earth. Their thighs had turned to mush and could not carry them, but they walked on anyway, along the shoulder of the streambed. They had barely covered a hundred yards when a shotgun explosion blasted the rocks at their feet and made sawdust of Guily's guitar.

"Acuesta te en el suelo!" a voice screamed. "Pon tus manos detras de tu cabeza!"

Cyril Divakov threw himself on the frozen dirt. It was close to a minute before his heart began to beat again. Two men jumped from the rocks. They looked like cowboys, well-fed and big-boned, wearing coats of sheep skin and Stetson hats, and holding rifles. One was Latin, Moctezuma (Mocty to his companion), with a thin beard and blue skin. The other one, Childs, was blond and pink and his eyes shined red when they caught light. They had lost their way after Childs had driven their jeep into a sea of mud during the blizzard; it now sat on its side at the other end of the canyon.

The men wanted to know the citizenship of Cyril Divakov and Guily, and Cyril Divakov lied, under Guily's terrified gaze, that they were American. He began to explain that they were backpackers who had escaped into the desert to cleanse their souls from the monotony of everyday life, but as he spoke blood pounded against the walls of his head and tears of terror burned his eyes. A premonition told him that his mission had exploded like a bag of popcorn.

Mocty unearthed Cyril Divakov's foreign passport.

"Are you aware of the punishment for entering the United States illegally or for lying about your citizenship?"

There was a kindness in his voice that rang with a string of terror. Cold moisture contracted around Cyril Divakov's testicles.

"Don't be afraid!" Mocty noticed. "We're not monsters."

They were Minutemen, a civilian militia who stalked the border and apprehended illegal immigrants.

"We guard the borders of our country because the government quit giving a damn," Mocty explained.

From Cyril Divakov's backpack they pulled out a stash of credit cards, a California driver's license and a notebook of rocket trajectory plans. He tried to explain that those were the pages of his dissertation, the calculations for the deployment of his mirrors across the cosmos, but his tongue was dry and stuck to his pallet.

"I wonder," Childs said, "what kind of undocumented students cross the asshole of geography loaded with credit cards and missile plans."

The Minutemen tied Cyril Divakov and Guily with climbing rope and ate all of their beef jerky. The tent was raised but the two captives were left out. Screaming at it brought them only hoarse throats. Cyril Divakov's legs were free but chances were it was a pretext for the Minutemen to shoot him in flight. He should have spat in their faces when there had been a chance.

"Goddamn country!" Guily cried. "Someone should run an airplane into this pile of dirt!"

"Don't take it out on the country, brother," Cyril Divakov said. "People still think big here, even our enemies, when the rest of the world fights over a bone and a puddle to drink from."

He had no cover other than his wet coat, and when the pain from the cold became unbearable he passed out. When the morning sun tickled him awake and he heard the gurgle of melting snow, he was surprised to be alive. The sky was blue and the walls of the canyon glistened with new water.

"Do you know what the power of the Minutemen is, boys?" Childs said. He had been waiting for them to wake up. "Flexibility and passion. We are not slaves of politicking and we love our country to death." He rubbed his teeth clean with toothpaste and a finger, and spat out the mixture.

"I've been wrestling with a question," he went on. "How do we distinguish if a border-crosser isn't in truth an even uglier element, like a terrorist funded to produce missiles on our own front lawn? If I were one, I'd surely come in by the coyote routes. Nobody's looking for me here, am I right or am I right?"

It was enough rope for Cyril Divakov to hang himself. He pled his case that he was a doctor of science, that all he cared about was creating a fail-proof system to let us see back to the beginning of time, and still the Minutemen refused to understand. The sun pounded his bare head and his migraine returned. Despair crept over his skin like a rash. After six hours of interrogation in which he wept, begged, cursed and threatened, he succumbed to their wishes, if only to save his sanity. He planned to destroy America by aiming shooting stars at its famous buildings, he told them, and by drowning its cities in stardust. At first they did not believe him, but he convinced them through the black flames in his eyes. Guily begged him to stop because he thought the Minutemen would kill them, but by then Cyril Divakov believed in his infernal plans more than his own accusers. When his account had crossed the line of good taste, a fist punched him in the chest and felled him on his back.

"Just like I was suspecting," Childs said.

Fingers handled Cyril Divakov's crotch and unzipped his pants. He was embarrassed by the pungent odor of his underwear: he had not changed it in five days of sweating and rationing toilet paper.

"The hobbit is not an Arab!" Childs said. "But it takes little to make him into one."

Cyril Divakov was startled to sense fingers touching his uncircumcised penis. They peeled and rubbed the sensitive head and a Swiss Army knife changed hands. He screamed and tried to see where it went but Mocty leaned on his head. Cyril Divakov begged them not to hurt him, he cried like a sick child and his mouth filled with a foul breath. A monsoon of tears poured out without permission. Shame, rage, a pathetic impotence and a numbing sense of doom tore his guts. His bowels expelled feces and his urine flowed onto the hands of Childs, who began thrusting them to cast off the filth.

"Goddamn savage! I should've castrated you for real!"

Cyril Divakov lay on his back with his eyes wide open. In the outskirts of his mind a flock of ravens circled the sky in anguish. A deep rumble approached and made the earth shudder as if from a bad omen, before it dissipated for a moment. The mountain reclaimed a nervous silence. A few seconds later, the yellow rocks stepped back in fear, a rattler slid behind a cactus, and Mocty's stomach made a gurgling noise. Then—a frothing torrent of mud and boulders crashed through the canyon with the speed of a curse. It swept the tent and the people and shot them across the narrows where the surge rose to a height of two hundred feet and jammed mounds of debris between the rock walls.

As the mud carried him off, Cyril Divakov prepared to enjoy the peace promised by his imminent death and used the time to compose a speech of apology to his mother. She would be sad, since seeing him would ruin her belief in his immortality. And astrophysics, his seductress, would be lost forever. The very idea of it threw a dagger into his heart. It was not a small detail to consider. Could it be the signature of a real man to abandon his dreams in mid-stride, to quit with such facility? He was close to figuring it out when the current of mud lifted him toward the heavens and slammed him against the rocks.

He woke up hanging like a bat from a ball of debris logged three stories up into the air. A few twists of his feet and gravity sent him plummeting toward the solid earth, when Guily materialized underneath and caught Cyril Divakov in his arms.

"I found my guitar," the Frenchman said. "It has been blown off to smithereens and is completely unusable."

By reason or whim, Cyril Divakov should have fled then and there. Why risk falling into the hands of enemies a second time? Why taunt fate again? True and true, but surviving the onslaught of nature had given him evidence of his own invincibility. Wet and freezing, he spent the day excavating up and down the canyon with the resolve of a grave robber. Guily followed him around, demanding to know what they were still doing in this cursed wasteland. But how could Cyril Divakov explain? His pride demanded that he prove to his enemies he was doing nothing bad, to teach them a lesson about the civilized treatment of human beings.

Pieces of Childs were scattered across a mile of mud, while Mocty clutched to life with two broken legs and a concussion. Cyril Divakov dragged the living man to higher ground and pulled his eyelids open. "Do you want to know now why I'm here?"

"You want to be a squatter in my country," Mocty said.

Cyril Divakov leaned forward until their noses touched. "You despise me, but in ten years in America I accomplished more than you can dream of in two lifetimes."

"I don't despise you," Mocty said. "I love my country, that's all. If a bum breaks into your house and eats your kids' food, do you let him sleep with your wife, too?"

"I have a doctorate from the most prestigious science university in the world, which waived its entire tuition to have me!"

"Maybe they did. All you have to show is a deportation stamp."

Cyril Divakov kicked Mocty's broken leg. Mocty choked from the pain but remained conscious. His eyes filled with tears and he scanned the harsh terrain with tenderness.

"The Apache used to spend the summers here," Mocty said. "You can still hear their voices inside the caves. And right over the mountain, down that gulch, there's a place called Sweet Water. The settlers that came, they knew a good joke when they saw one—the place is nothing but a dry lake covered with salt. You can still trace their tracks there. Sometimes they vanish in the middle, as if the people got snatched by aliens—it's where gunslingers would ambush them for gold. Bones are scattered all over those parts. The rattlers nest on them now."

Cyril Divakov picked up some snow and sucked on it. He didn't want to hear any of this.

"It is a mythical land, this place you're trespassing on," Mocty said. "We had to know your plans."

Cyril Divakov snorted a laugh and felt sick.

"We were not going to hurt you," Mocty added.

"Liar!" Cyril Divakov screamed. The image of the blade reaching for his organ flashed before him. His eyes turned wet. He felt Mocty's reassuring hand on his and jerked away. Mocty's face filled with great pity. "You cannot understand me because you despise your own country."

Cyril Divakov hit him but shook with weakness, like a parent confronting his child's murderer. His eyes watered and his muscles ached. He couldn't conceal the anger that was eating him. What was he doing here? What sick vanity had convinced him to seek the approval of a minion like Mocty? A man has to be tough, not only with himself but with the world around him. When life swings at you, you swing back. It was time to leave, away from this place, far from this day.

Mocty begged them to take him: there was no food except lizards and snakes and he would have to fight for them with the vultures and cougars. He would die from cold or gangrene or the jaws of a beast.

"A man like you should know how to lie in the bed he's made for himself." Cyril Divakov cut him off and walked away. Guily followed.

For hours they scrambled over debris and waded in cesspools of green water that stunk of animal carcasses. The mud stole Cyril Divakov's boots and he continued barefoot. His clothes dried and his body gained warmth and then the sun set and he was cold again. He tried to stay focused on tomorrow's promises, but the canyon behind him cut into his thoughts like an ingrown nail. And what was there to think twice about? Mocty had invited his own black fortune through his spite and prejudice. When had Cyril Divakov hurt the man—or any other fascist like him? He had salvaged Mocty out of the mud, when anybody with half a brain would have let him rot. So why was Cyril Divakov standing trial before his own conscience for refusing to save that reptile?

Black darkness had buried the Earth by the time the mountain ended. Wind hit the two men from many directions and a sky of stars opened ahead. It was a night of agony that could freeze a man's spit. Even after the sun materialized on the next morning, the scale barely touched thirty. Cyril Divakov woke up before Guily. Behind him were the mountains they had crossed and ahead lay a vast desert where a man could breathe again. The earth around him was white and tasted like salt because they had reached the ancient lakebed of Sweet Water. The jeep that Mocty and Childs had abandoned lay on its side in a puddle of brine. Bones bleached by the sun were strewn until the eye could see. Cyril Divakov stepped on them and found them stronger than steel and more flexible than hard rubber, because the obstinacy of the men they had once belonged to had made them indestructible.

The wild emptiness touched Cyril Divakov; it made him human again for the first time since his deportation. It was worth suffering a thousand and one nights of torture just to let his mind loose in a land this big—but he had to enter it free of fear and a guilty heart. A knot of anguish was squeezing his guts and spoiling his enjoyment of liberty. He stretched his eyes until he could see over the curvature of the earth, to where the freeway traffic was crawling along like a procession of ants. He knitted bones into a complication of levers and lifted the jeep. The engine rumbled on but could not wake up Guily, who was sleeping in a coma of exhaustion. Cyril Divakov drew a big arrow in the salt and wrote: "Drive until you reach the freeway and turn left."

On the trail back into the mountains, his heart beat against his chest with such vigor that he paused often to make sure it had not cracked a rib. By the time the sun weighed over the peaks, he had found Mocty surrounded by vultures. Cyril Divakov threw a rock at the scavengers and they retreated, provisionally and without conviction.

"Tell me, border-crosser," Mocty asked, "how far do you think you'll get with this goddamn back and forth?"

Cyril Divakov blew off black mucus from his nose and gave Mocty a hand.

"All the way," he said.

He lifted Mocty on his shoulders and started the long way back to Sweet Water. The last rays of the sun threw heat on him and the air smelled of wet earth. His bare feet were bleeding and his back threatened to collapse but he did not need them to go on. His mind was flying ahead, to the end of the mountain, along the freeway, through the streets of Los Angeles, behind the lenses of telescopes and across the universe. The fears, doubts and guilt he had worn like birthmarks had fled, for the moment, not because he had defeated them with reason, but because he had scared them away with his infuriating stubbornness to keep on dreaming.

The fears, doubts and guilt he had worn like birthmarks had fled, for the moment, not because he had defeated them with reason, but because he had scared them away with his infuriating stubbornness to keep on dreaming.

Ernest Farrés
Two Poems on Edward Hopper's Paintings

Translated from Catalan
by Lawrence Venuti

RAILROAD TRAIN, 1908

No sooner is the caboose
out of sight than they've
already forgotten you.
It's like losing clout or taking
a load off their minds. That's just
how they, who are out
to lunch or do nothing
with their lives, wash their hands
of you. Got it? Yet the trains you catch
are determined, air-conditioned, carnivorous,
in fine fettle. Thickening fogs
rise yet fail to intimidate them.
They breathe in, breathe out, iridesce, seethe.
They need a ton of room
to levitate in a hurry, heading
for the possibility of other worlds
or an extraordinary order of things.
Their windows give evidence of valleys,
depressions.

Leaving on days beneath a leaden sky
is true to type, as if clouds were formed through contact
with sweat and hot breath.
                              Hours later
you'll be swaddled in strange lights and shadows,
gusts and twittering colors, unaccustomed racket.

SUMMERTIME, 1943

The girl from the house with the stone stoop
has gone out into the street
swaying her body
just as she does every morning.
You know what? You know why they come to me
these crazy desires
to rest my insomniac
eyes on her?
You know why I lose my north
when I see her pull up
to come face to face with the summer
light? Or why she appears
in my dreams
among white petunias?
The act of checking out
the girl from the house with the stone stoop
painstakingly
is my way of sparing myself:
1. From killing time, searching out the corner

of my eye through half the sun-blasted city
for people who are artichoke hearts or creeps,
girls who turn pale along with their lives,
some clown with a briefcase or dog-tired workers
far from Pyrrho, Gorgias and those who proclaim,
"The seizure of power by the proletariat
leads to perpetuating that power which, corrupted,
passes to other hands and that's all she wrote!"
raising their voices in vain.
2. From cutting ties between my psyche
and reality, both of them a hard business.
If that happened, I'd shy away from the world
like a toad, vegan on the fringe of life's pleasures,
passive while others rid themselves of acrimony
by dint of watching
the girl from the house
with the stone stoop.
3. From finally realizing that I'm deluded,
that my whole life is a cock-and-bull story,
that the frustrations, right moments,
attempts to get out of a tight spot
and even the girl from the house

David McGlynn
Wanderers In Zion

The trail switches through a small riparian stand of cottonwoods and then rises out of the shade into a terrain that knows no water. The piñons are hardened against the heat and thrust forward in the afternoon sun like stage props under a spotlight. The rock-slide to the ridge is a long tongue of loose debris; each step is like climbing a staircase in an abandoned house, the floor shifting and slightly fluid beneath our feet. Most of the hike has been like this, nine miles along the Virgin River through the Great West Canyon of Zion National Park, impossible passageways and dangerous scrambles across unsteady ground. After nine hours I have grown only slightly accustomed to it.

We ascend until we come to a gap in the ridge wide enough for a foot to anchor. I pull myself up and then turn to pull Katherine, who I've been dating for the past year, and Jenny, and finally, Joe, his big hand curling around my wrist. I lean back to cantilever against his weight. When he's up, I turn and look around. Before us spreads an empty grassland mesa, west onto nothing, no parking lot, no cars, no road. The wash to the south is as steep as the canyon wall. If I had a map, I'd be able to name the wash and the two peaks on the periphery of our view. I'd see that we'd climbed out too early. Without a map, however, I can't name anything, not even my mistake. "Uh oh," Katherine says.

"Should we turn around?" Jenny asks.

"Now that we're out of the canyon that doesn't make much sense," Joe says. He's a gray-bearded, big-gutted, retired cop from Minneapolis. We met him on the trail an hour ago; he was separated from his hiking group, as we were from ours.

"Maybe the parking lot is in a ways," I say. "We need to hike in to find the trail."

None of us, however, realizes how far off course we've strayed. A winding access road skirts the perimeter of the wilderness between the lower and upper trailheads. The road curves sharply east as it climbs from the canyon and then immediately tracks several miles to the west. Hiking west, as instinct tells us to do, will lead us parallel to the road rather than perpendicular to it. We don't realize the right trail out of the canyon is two miles farther downriver than where we ascended. And now that we're above the canyon rim, we can see the thunderhead building in the southwest corner of the sky. There's no telling if it'll hit us, but if it does, it's sure to be a heavy, late-summer monsoon. Even a small rain can cause a flash flood in the canyon, those tumbling brown-and-white avalanches of water that scythe off trees and deposit boulders at Martian-like angles. Hiking in a canyon or down-climbing on loose gravel is no place to be when that happens.

"I'm really nervous about this," Jenny says.

"It's fine," I say. "Our best option."

"I need to pray before we go on," Jenny says. She turns her back to us and lowers her head, knits her fingers together and holds them at her waist. Her green shorts ride high on her hips. Her lips move, but she doesn't utter a sound.

I stand beside Katherine, but I'm careful not to stand too close. When I look her way, I gather her in with quick, furtive glances—the glittery dust on her calves, the dark outline of her purple bikini top through her T-shirt—then turn to study the rocks and sky. I'm afraid that if Jenny catches me staring, she'll know what I've been trying all day to hide.

"You guys Mormon?" Joe asks.

"No," I say.

"What are you then?"

"We're evangelicals," Jenny says, coming back to us. "We're hiking with a group from our church. Up in Salt Lake City."

"Oh," Joe says.

Katherine stays quiet. She doesn't like "evangelical," and to be honest, neither do I. Literally, it means "bringer of good news," which sounds all right—hope for the despairing, rescue for the oppressed, sustenance for the starved. As an adjective, the word has been used to describe Protestants on both the left and the right, and even some Catholics. As a noun, "evangelical" demarcates a far narrower subset of Christians, a group who has received so much attention in recent years that certain images have become iconic: ultra-modern churches with worship centers the size of concert arenas; services outfitted with electric instruments and JumboTron screens; throngs of ecstatic believers jumping up and down or swaying en masse with their palms opened above their heads and tears streaming down their cheeks.

I have swayed with my eyes open and closed, in megachurches from coast to coast and across the Pacific, but "evangelical" is not a word I use to describe myself. I prefer "nondenominational," or else to dismiss the idea of category altogether. I tell people I'm not religious, but am, rather, relational: shorthand for the idea that my brand of Christianity cuts away every liturgical and canonical tradition, every division between Protestants and Catholics (though we're decidedly Protestant), between Calvinists and Wesleyans, dispenses with every candle and vestment, every specter of religiosity and instead interacts directly with Jesus—so true a form of religion it transcends the very word. "Nondenominational" sounds more modern, as though denominations are the factions of the dry-lipped and white-haired. It also sounds less loaded—not so Jerry Falwell, not so Jim and Tammy Faye.

The year I turned fifteen, I talked my mother into letting me spend the summer with my father and stepmother in California. I'd go for ten weeks rather than the three decreed by the divorce settlement. I needed a break from Houston. My closest friend had been killed in a home invasion, and I couldn't face another summer of mowing lawns and lifeguarding in the Texas heat. My mother hoped that by allowing me to go, I wouldn't want to stay there for good. She warned me to put such ideas out of my head.

My stepmother was a children's pastor at an evangelical church in Orange County, by no means the largest church in the area—some of the largest churches in the country are headquartered there—but large enough to have its own education building, which I spent several weeks painting. When that was finished, I rolled posters and shrink-wrapped prints for a local artist. I dug out a long strip of rock-hard cheatgrass from the backside of a carpenter's workshop. I didn't have any friends, and I didn't mind. I went to the beach every afternoon, and on my days off, I rode with my father to his sales calls. He sold printing to big companies and his calls ranged from Sherman Oaks to Oceanside. I was happy to go with him wherever he went.

He had disappeared so quickly. The divorce had taken nearly a year, but it was a year of shifting recriminations and false hopes. Even while my parents hired lawyers and began cataloging the contents of our house, and my sister and I spent every other weekend sleeping on the floor of the apartment my father shared with two other divorced men, we held out hope that they would reconcile. We ate dinner together on Sundays, as a family. My father and mother took long walks along the bayou behind our house. They bought a car. Then it was over and my father was gone and my mother went about filling in the empty space he left behind. Within weeks a man moved into our house. He hung his clothes in my father's closet and slept in my father's side of the bed, on the same mattress and the same linens. Early mornings, gray light through the blinds, I'd look in their room and see two lumps beneath the bedspread, and for a moment it felt as though everything had been a dream. Except I knew better. By the time my sister and I flew to California for Christmas, my mother was engaged, and by our first summer, she was married. She talked of my stepfather adopting my sister and me, of us taking his name.

My father listened to talk radio whenever he was in the car. Even before he met my stepmother and became born-again, my father had liked talk shows, liked banter and argument, liked talk, but back then the talk was mostly about strategies for selling and motivating corporate teams. Now the talk was about the perils of the country. He listened to Rush Limbaugh and Dr. Laura and then punched over to the Christian station and listened to Chuck Smith and James Dobson. They all said more or less the same things. America had grown too permissive, too liberal, and its traditional foundations were eroding. Soon the well of grace would run dry. Nations that turned away from God would be turned away by Him.

My father's Honda Prelude sat so low to the ground I sometimes imagined him changing lanes by sliding the car between the tires of a semi-trailer and emerging on the other side. He kept the radio loud to drown out the traffic noise. Now and then he'd say "good point" or else gesture to the radio dial and then look at me as if to say, "You hear that?" But most of the time he just listened and bobbed his head. In this way I was catechized into the Gemini worlds of evangelicalism and conservativism, the two so closely braided together I couldn't tell them apart. I believed Rush to be a Christian because he lined up with the Christians, and likewise, that it was "Christian" to laugh-off evolution as a hair-brained theory and to scoff at the idea of chlorofluorocarbons from hairspray canisters having anything to do with the hole in the ozone layer. Or that there even was a hole in the ozone layer.

Anyone who's ever read *The Divine Comedy* knows the seven Christian virtues—humility, kindness, forgiveness, diligence, charity, temperance and chastity—are ordered from the most important to the least, in antithesis to the seven deadly sins—pride, envy, wrath, sloth, greed, gluttony and lust. Because pride is the deadliest sin, humility is the greatest virtue. Listening to talk radio in my father's car, however, I learned a different order of virtue. I learned precisely the *opposite* order. Lust is the gravest of sins and thus, abortion and homosexuality are the gravest evils. I learned a host of other problems—teenage pregnancy, pornography, domestic violence, AIDS, divorce—were the consequences of a cultural devaluing of chastity. History contained abundant examples of great men brought low by lust, men who turned to duplicity and rage in order to satisfy their sexual appetites. The chaste man, on the other hand, embodied all the other virtues. The chaste man was most tempered, for he was practiced in the art of self-restraint; the chaste man was most charitable, for he understood that sexual intimacy is a gift given only in marriage; the chaste man was most diligent, habituated to toiling against the heat of his own desires; the chaste man was most forgiving, slow to anger as he was slow to passion; the chaste man was most kind, denying himself the apparatus of envy by knowing no other bodies besides his spouse's; the chaste man was most humble, for he resisted the wiles and scorn of the world and sojourned through youth and into adulthood a misfit—a resister of temptation, an alien to sex.

My stepmother's daughter spent two weeks at a summer camp for pre-college teens in Colorado Springs analyzing "major worldviews" in light of a Christian perspective. She arrived home with a suitcase filled with books about how Oliver North was a scapegoat in the Iran-Contra affair, how feminism derived from Communism, and how most of the music she enjoyed, including the Beatles and Prince and Quiet Riot, were lascivious and Satanic. The afternoon of her return, my stepsister cut most of her cassettes in half with a pair of scissors. When we went out to dinner to welcome her home, she announced she'd awakened as a Christian. It wasn't enough to believe, she said. She'd use her college degree to work for the kingdom. My stepmother began to cry, then rose from her seat, circled the table, and kissed her. My father smiled. He'd come through a difficult time and was in a good place again.

I smiled, too. It was a Saturday night and beyond the restaurant's windows the sun was setting over the Newport pier and boardwalk and the entire blue horizon of the Pacific. The wind through the open doors smelled of salt and sunscreen, and I could hear the valet attendants shouting as they shuffled the cars. We all ordered the same pasta dish and when our plates were taken away, the waiter brought out silver cups of spumoni. It felt like family, even if my mother and sister weren't a part of it. We were happy, and our happiness had been wrought by Jesus, the source of all things good and dependable. And a life *without* Jesus meant a life of fear—a high-wire walk across a treacherous ravine in which a single misstep meant not just a fall into the hell that follows death, but the hell of an unprotected life. The hell of murder. The hell of impermanent family. The hell of loneliness. All those hells were at bay and my step-sister's cassettes were in the garbage. It seemed to me a fair trade.

We stop and pass around the water bottle, a gray, transparent Nalgene that's been rid-ing all day in the meshed webbing of my pack. The water line is halfway up the hash marks, about twenty ounces' worth. I shake the bottle and hold it to the sky, hoping the sunlight passing through the water will cause it to multiply. Floating specks of dust and saliva bend into the redshift, tinting the water faintly violet. It's still as hot as noon, but once the sun loses the horizon the temperature will plummet. My socks are still damp from the hours we hiked through the river, and I can feel blisters forming on my toes and heels. I unscrew the cap and sip and pass the bottle. We each take only enough to kill the thirst, a communion's portion. No one must be told to take less. I replace the cap and slide the bottle back against my hip and we stand and argue.

Jenny wants to go back. She thinks we can manage the slide and the downclimb. "It's not that far from the rim to the trail," she says. "And it's a way we know." I'm tempted to declare myself licked and backtrack, though it's after five now and if we turn back, even under the best circumstances, we won't hit the canyon floor until eight and by then it will be pitch black. Lightning strikes in silence over the western mountains, followed twenty seconds later by a low rumble, like an unlatched car trunk bouncing down an unpaved road. I feel it in my chest.

Joe reaches down and hikes up his Neoprene knee brace. He presses his finger into the soft, livid flesh bunched over his kneecap. The skin whitens around his fingertip. "My struts won't make it down." He looks at me. "I'm too big to piggy back."

"That settles it," I say. "We hike on."

"Maybe I'll go back," Jenny says. "If I can get back to the trail, I can find my way out. You three can keep going."

"No," I say. I look her in the face so she knows I'm no longer talking to everyone. It is because of Jenny we got separated from our group in the first place; she took off alone and Katherine and I went after her. "We hike together. No one's going off alone."

We ascend a little knoll covered in dry tamarisk, like whiskers of pale straw, and scoot down the other side. The wash shallows out there and at the bottom we spot a stand of cottonwoods, all shadow and shade. Between the trunks I see a brown rectangular sign, facing away from us, held aloft by a green metal stake. "Look at that," I say. "That's got to be a trail marker." I point my shoes downhill and skid down the gully. The juniper scratches at my thighs and my socks fill with thorns, but I don't slow up. Jenny's fast behind me, tiny avalanches from her feet flowing around my shoes as I step and slide. Katherine and Joe descend more slowly. I get to the bottom and come around the sign and see that it bears the logo of the National Park Service, the cypress tree and mountain peak on an inverted arrowhead. It's not a trail marker. The stake marks the boundary of the park. On the other side is land governed by the Bureau of Land Management, earmarked for natural gas drilling and winter grazing leases, unpatrolled and untouched all the way to Nevada. Facing the sign, I'm standing outside Zion.

"This isn't the way," Joe calls out, side-stepping down the slope. "The gully won't lead us out."

"It could lead back into the canyon," Jenny says. "An easier way back to the trail."

"It's hard to say what's between here and there," Joe says. "If we get stuck, we'll be awfully hard to find down there."

"I'm just tired of this," Jenny says. "It's been three hours, my underwear's all up my butt, and I'm tired of it."

"Back up," I say. "Damn it."

We climb back up, pulling on the trunks of the cottonwoods to keep from backsliding, and I feel the panic beginning to wave in, each sweep climbing a little farther up the beach of my reason. Once I'm swamped, who knows what will happen. I've heard of bodies found naked in the desert, clothes folded into neat little piles beside them. I've heard of people who died with their own flesh clenched in their teeth. Will that be me? Will we wander until I lose my senses and begin to howl at the moon? I try to focus on what I know now: this hill, this ascent. I follow the backs of Jenny's knees. Dark veins spider across the creases between her calf and thigh. Her socks are caked in mud, and I can hear her crying softly. "This is my fault," she says. Exertion prevents her from sobbing louder. "This is all my fault. How did I get us into this mess?"

I'm winded, too, so I don't argue. But in my heart I know Jenny is wrong. It's not her fault we're lost. It's mine.

On a hot night at the end of July, Katherine and I went to a party for a friend moving out of state. The sky above the mountains throbbed orange and black. South of Provo, a forest was burning. The branches of the oak in the backyard were adorned with hanging paper lanterns, each intricately lettered with Japanese characters and lit from the inside by a small bulb. An orange extension cord wrapped the trunk of the tree and snaked toward the kitchen door through a disordered assembly of chairs. By the back steps of the house stood a folding table crowded with bottles, its downhill legs not quite snapped tight. One of the bottles was Belvedere Vodka, which I like because it's expensive and don't often drink for the same reason. I scooped ice into a red plastic cup big enough for a beer, filled it halfway with vodka and added a splash of Seven-Up. I drained it and poured a second. This one I sipped more slowly, sitting in a lawn chair while the oak listed and creaked in the wind.

The music was loud, coming from a boom box propped in the kitchen window. Contrails of smoke drifted across the sky and the wind smelled like an extinguished match. The stars appeared to fall through the oak leaves and land on my shirt. I was washed in starlight, in golden haloes from the feet of the lanterns, and smoke, and when I lifted my hand to touch it—touch this dazzling, star-spangled firmament—my hand appeared to drag along in time. I closed my eyes tight and when I reopened them the firmament was still there and I understood I wasn't hallucinating. I was drunk.

Katherine drifted across the yard, her sandals sloughing through the weeds. She stopped and turned her eyes to me. I stood and went for her. "I'm hammered," I said. "You've got to get me out of here before I make an ass of myself."

"I've had a few myself," she said.

"Can you drive?"

"Probably," she said. "For a while at least."

Her jeep was parked on the street. The top was off, so I stepped up onto the rear tire, took hold of the roll bar and swung into the backseat. "I'll sit here," I said. Katherine started the engine and took a head-clearing breath before releasing the brake. A Salt Lake City native, she knew the roads where the police were least likely to park, the winding shortcuts along streets without lamps. I leaned my head against the spare tire bolted against the rear and watched the stars turn in the sky. The moon rose and sank, as though the entire night was passing in minutes. The Milky Way was three-dimensional. The jeep climbed a hill and swung around a corner. I felt like I was on a roller coaster with my hands in the air. I looked forward and could only see Katherine's hair whipping around the headrest.

We parked in front of my house. Katherine held my arm as I jumped to the lawn.

I fumbled my keys out of my pocket and tossed them to her. She dropped them on the grass and bent to collect them and when she leaned up we were laughing. We made our way, laughing, toward the door and through it, and through the house to my bedroom. We fell down laughing on the bed, drunk and in love for more than a year without having done anything more than kiss. We kissed. My roommate was gone and we kissed with impunity, the lights on and the blinds open. At first our kissing was playful, but all at once it turned serious, two gears higher, as though we'd come to the end of our little country road of affection and merged onto a new interstate of touch. I felt her belly in my hands, her breasts, and before either of us remembered to stop, our clothes were tangled up together on the floor.

It happens a billion times a day—people coming together like this. How many other couples left the party and ended up this way? I was twenty-five and the last of my kind. My friends from college were married. My few previous girlfriends were married. My non-evangelical friends had shucked off their innocence long ago. I was the only one left, and I was in love. I was in love, and every event in my life, every victory and disappointment, every yes and every no, felt like a prologue to this instant. My heart hammered so hard it made me queasy. The swamp cooler clanked in the window down the hallway. I pressed my eyebrows against Katherine's. Her lashes made a faint wind against my cornea. I leaned back and saw her silver necklace pooled into the hollow of her throat, like a coiled rope. She bit her lip and I saw she was afraid. I was afraid, too. We could still turn back. We could say we drank too much. And though it may be true that the vodka loosened my inhibitions, I want the record to show I was not, at the moment the decision was made, drunk. I was conscious of and responsible for everything. I could have stopped as I'd stopped so many times before. I looked at the hair sweeping across Katherine's forehead, the tiny crinkles where her nose met her cheeks, the hardly-visible delta of veins in her chin, and I saw the illuminated path of my future. I reached out and touched the life I'd been waiting years to begin.

Only afterward did I remember my old promises and inhabit the fears of what would happen now that I'd broken them. I watched Katherine disentangle her clothes from mine with a kind of terror, worried that this one instance of coming together would become the spark of our estrangement. After all those years of hearing how God returns misfortune for sin, punishing men and nations alike, how could I think I was any different?

I didn't say any of this to Katherine as I walked her out to the jeep. We held each other and kissed in a hesitant way, as though we'd witnessed a tragedy. We kissed because we didn't want the night to feel empty. And because it *wasn't* empty. The mountains were veiled behind a curtain of fog, and moisture beaded on my arms. I was shivering. I leaned in to kiss her once more, but before my lips touched hers, I said maybe we should go on the hiking trip with the group from church. We'd agreed to stay home that weekend, but I was changing my mind. A weekend with other "strong Christians" would be good for us, I said. Help us avoid future sins.

We kick the stones out of the tamarisk, stamp the ground flat and sit down in a circle. My right knee rubs against Joe's, my left against Katherine's. It is Katherine I shuffle away from. We unzip our packs and take inventory: half a pouch of Jack Links beef jerky, a plastic jar filled with raisins and peanuts and M&Ms, and a Ziploc baggie of gummy bears. It's more than I expected, and miraculously dry despite being dipped in the river throughout the day. We pass the jerky around and each pull out a chew, like a strip of tree bark. Jenny dumps the gummy bears into her hand, lays the baggie flat on the ground and spreads the bears on the plastic. She leans over her crossed legs as she counts. "Thirty-eight bears," she says. "Nine a piece, with two left over for the men."

"We get extra?" Joe asks.

"You're bigger, you need more. We need to ration anyway. Three now, three in the morning, save three for later tomorrow."

"Jenny, they're gummy bears," Katherine says. "They have, like, ten calories each."

"We still need to think about what we'll eat tomorrow."

I fish three M&Ms from the jar and cradle them in my palm. I stare down at the three colored eggs nesting against my lifelines, and wonder if the end of my story is already foretold in the creases of my hand. I know nothing of astrology, glean no meaning from my sign or the signs of others and lack any ability to decipher the secrets inscribed in my skin. What I do know is people die out here. It happens every year. Last autumn, two women went for a day hike in the mountains east of Salt Lake City, an early snowstorm struck, and they weren't found until spring. Just some tattered clothing and a few bear-licked bones.

Before I can gobble down the M&Ms, Jenny asks if we should pray. Joe shrugs, "Be my guest." Jenny and Katherine look to me, perhaps because I'm male but more likely because I'm known to pray aloud during Bible study. I set the M&Ms on my pack and close my eyes. "Lord," I say, "thank you for this food. Help us have the strength to keep hiking. Help us find the road." It's enough of a prayer for now, a little prayer for little food, but rather than saying "Amen," I keep talking. I ask for forgiveness for our arrogance in thinking we could find our way without God's guidance, for not praying the moment we got lost. I pray for all our unrepented sins, for all our lusts and hungers. Jesus lived for forty days without food; surely we can endure a night on three gummy bears and a strip of jerky. Then, still sputtering half-coherent platitudes about Christ's ordeal in the desert, I start to think of Katherine, the hollow point of her neck, the silver chain in a coil. I try to evade the thoughts, but they won't go away. I speak faster and soon my prayer becomes a chant, words flowing over words like water over stone. I feel as though I'm rising above myself, looking down at the tops of our heads and our packs in a circle. I no longer feel the ground. I promise God if we make it out of here, I'll give up every fleshly desire, every bodily need. I'll cut ties with the world and all its trappings. I'll never touch Katherine again.

It is a promise I know I cannot keep. I have crossed into another country, one where my old language and currency won't get me very far. I've tried to convince myself that what happened with Katherine was the result of a lapse in faith; I sought my will before God's and fell into sin. Now I see it was a symptom not of a momentary lapse but of a much larger fracturing. My convictions are changing shape, like an origami crane being unfolded and smoothed flat and folded again into a different animal. For months I've squirmed during Bible study, and Katherine has, too, arguing about whether women should teach men or hold positions in the pastorate, or whether a vapor canopy covered the Earth in the days before the Fall. Katherine volunteers with Planned Parenthood, and I coach a gay swimming team two nights a week. As my friendships with the men and women on the team have deepened, I've come to feel embarrassed about being a part of a church that doesn't welcome them. I'm embarrassed by the swaying and singing, by the strobe lights and rock music, by the braiding together of religion and politics. And I've tried for years to believe a heart could be so filled with *agape* it no longer required *eros*, that it could go without touch, or late-night phone conversations in the dark, or clandestine meals in out-of-the-way diners. Now, lost in the desert, I knew I could not, and moreover would not, go without any of those things. The body and soul have different needs and one cannot take the place of the other.

As if aware of my every thought, or maybe to prod me to shut up so we can eat, Katherine sets her hand on my knee. Her palm is gritty and her heat radiates up my thigh. I cup my hand over hers and tighten my grip until I feel her pulse in my hand, and with the same inner voice with which I moments ago promised never to touch her again, I tell God to leave me out here all night. Set me to wander this desert for all eternity. Lay me down to sleep beneath the juniper tree night after hungry night and still I will not let go.

When we get back to Salt Lake City, Katherine and I will sit on my couch, and cry, and finally admit that we can no longer go back to the church. We are no longer evangelicals, and we've known it for a while, though our day of wandering will come to reside as the moment we at last understood it. After so many years and so many people I've known and loved—so many nights with my forehead pressed to the floor in fervent communion with a God who felt as though he sat beside me—it is not easy to part with an old life. It's not simply a matter of enlightenment, of wising-up. It's rather a mournful resignation reminiscent of the night my father and mother at last agreed to divorce. My father drove out to the house, but didn't come all the way inside. He and my mother talked in the entryway. I listened from the laundry room and my sister was in her bedroom. My mother and father's voices were matter-of-fact and when they finished, my mother said, "Okay, I'll tell them." As though we didn't already know. My father left without saying hello or goodbye to us. I could hear my sister crying when my mother opened her bedroom door. When she came into the laundry room, I kept my back turned and moved the clothes from the washer to the dryer.

I made it out of the desert, but I often feel as though I'm still wandering there. I've drifted between a number of different churches over the years, innocuous denominations that don't cause people to raise their eyebrows when I say their names. I sip coffee after the service and learn the names of congregants and even take my turn reading the scriptures on Sunday mornings. But I'm not part of the place in the way I used to be. I decline the invitations to attend the Bible studies or men's fellowship groups or weekend retreats. I tell myself I'm comfortable this way, my privacy uninvaded, my secrets unknown, but it's also unfortunate. I don't know anybody's passions and no one knows mine. No one has heard me holler or sing. I withhold until withholding makes me restless, until I relish the Sundays when I skip service to sleep and cook breakfast, until I convince myself I don't belong in that church, that *it isn't me*, that it's time to look elsewhere.

Wandering, though, has its own lessons to teach—lessons the Israelites had to learn again and again during their sojourn in Sinai: to trust the light in the sky; to give thanks for your food, no matter how little; to separate the comforts of the past from realities of the present, the qualifiers of faith from faith itself. Moses came down from Mount Sinai with the Ten Commandments not because his people didn't already know the rules, but because they needed to be reminded of them. How few things are inscribed in stone. I can recite the Lord's Prayer, the Nicene Creed, the Apostles' Creed, the Benediction, and I believe every word. I love church coffee and communion wine, stained glass and incense, Easter palms folded into crosses which children—as though aware of the faith's bloody history—flip upside down and brandish as swords. I am a Christian; it is one of the central nouns of my life. What I lack, what I continue to seek, are the adjectives.

And out by the highway is a big new evangelical church. The children's wing has a bank of windows four-stories tall and a marquis that looks like it belongs at Toys R' Us. On Sunday afternoons in the summer Katherine and I drive by it with the windows down, right when the evening service is starting up. We can hear the music going, the drummer's foot stomping on the bass, four thousand hands all coming together in unison, over and over again, like the great beating heart of the world. Our neighbors down the street, our librarian, the woman who sold us a garlic press at the mall—they are all clapping together, all calling out to God. The beat gets inside the windows and disrupts the radio. It's wild and rapturous and calls out to me. Beyond the church the highway opens up onto land not yet conquered, the empty desert earth, the Salt Flats shimmering on the horizon. I press the accelerator to the floor, headlong into the phantasms of heat, hoping to outrun the sound.

The remaining daylight is an orange smear over the western horizon when we gather up our small amount of trash and prepare to move on. I whisper to Katherine that we need to think soon about making a camp. She nods and whispers, "I know." I think of stacking dried juniper branches into a teepee and building a fire, spindling the spark with two sticks as though playing a cello, nursing the ember into a flame inside my cupped hands. I imagine the heart of the fire starting to beat, the tongues of flame strobing as we squat on our toes to absorb the warmth, our chins and teeth flickering with light and shadow. I imagine building a straw nest in the dirt and bedding down beside Katherine, tucking my knees into the backs of hers, her hair in my face. So long as we're lost, desperate and starved, I'm free to indulge in the immediate, to seek warmth and sustenance wherever I can find it.

We head toward a stand of trees in search of wood to burn, and when we come around the trees, we stumble into a grassy meadow filled with horses grazing on the tamarisk. The horses retreat into a circle until their tails touch. They stamp and whinny as we approach. We get around them and see an old fifth-wheel trailer tipped forward with its rusted hitch in the grass. The trailer's planks are wind-mottled, the white wheels inside the tires pocked with rust. "That didn't get here by helicopter," Joe says. "I'll bet this is a grazing lease. BLM land."

"That means we're out of the park?" I ask.

"Out of the park."

"Should we try to ride the horses out?"

"Bareback? Go ahead, give it your best shot."

The trailer is parked at the end of a narrow dirt path, the wheel ruts eroded by wind and rain. The path winds in a wide S, right and then left, and we arrive at a sunflower field. In late summer, unruffled by cold or snow or people, the flowers have grown over six feet. The heads are as big as clocks and bob in the cooling air, as though nodding in assent. It is that time that evades name between dusk and night when the gap between sunlight and moonlight makes the sky appear especially dark. So dark I don't see the people standing among the flowers until we nearly bump into them.

A man in a white shirt holds a little girl by the armpits, lifting her as she attempts to throw a leg over a horse. Another girl who looks about thirteen stands with an instamatic camera. Both girls wear their hair in braided pigtails and the same homemade, pastel-green prairie dress fastened tight at their collars and wrists.

"Hello!" I call out. The girls gasp and the older one hurries behind the man. The man lifts the little girl from the horse and sets her on the ground. He places his hand on the top of her head. "We're lost," I say.

"Not for long," he says. He has a high forehead and a skinny, creased neck. His glasses, made of thin, gold metal, are too wide for his face. "The road is a half-mile down."

"We're a ways from our car," I say. "You couldn't give us a lift, could you?"

"I suppose that'd be all right." We follow him down the trail to a green Dodge minivan idling with its headlights off. A boy, also in a white shirt and too young to drive, sits behind the wheel. The man slides open the side door and cranes his long neck inside. "Mother, these folks need a ride to their car. What do you think?"

The boy climbs out of the driver's seat and out of the van's belly step three women, two who look to be in their late teens or early twenties, and finally, a third, far older, closer in age to the man, her round plastic glasses several decades out of style. Her hair is styled in a sort of pompadour, with a French braid reaching to the center of her back. All three women wear the same green dress as the younger girls, buttoned from navel to neck, with stiff triangular collars, and pleated below the waist and ruffled at the shoulders, as though it's some sort of uniform. I quickly realize it *is* a uniform. They're polygamists, prevalent still in the forgotten strips of land between the state parks in southern Utah, occupying frontier-like towns on the Utah-Arizona border in order to evade the jurisdictions of either state. They're a reclusive people who don't cotton to strangers and don't like to be intruded upon. This is how they take their outings—down deserted roads at the end of twilight. I don't know if the two younger women who stepped out of the van are the man's daughters or his wives. I pray the youngest two know the man only as a father.

Mother stops at the door of the van, the dome light illuminating the gray strands in her braid. She hovers, half bent, not wanting to climb out. She holds her dress bunched in her fist. She crinkles her nose at the sight of my legs, at the bands of dirt and blood spiraling up my calves. She looks worried, as though suspecting me of some power to take away her husband, break up her family and disrupt her way of life; at the very least to judge and scorn her beliefs. Another me in another time and place would have judged her, but not now. The time for judgment has passed. "I won't be long," the man says. "Just wait right here." He extends his hand to her. She slides her fingers into his palm and floats to the ground. Her dress falls to within an inch of the earth. She steps past me and I say, "Thank you." She nods and I can't help saying it again, to her and her husband, to her son kicking rocks in the road, to her sister-wives and daughters, to her entire clan, "Thank you, thank you." My gratitude gushes like water from a rock. Once she's out of the way, I climb inside the van, ready to be delivered.

A.K. Scipioni
Picnic Ramallah

Married, the schoolboys make the shells
at night, parting their nails and triggers,
branding an emptied plain, and the pocks
of the empty plain, with powder and wax,
and the smell of clementines. The rolling

hills of Hezbollah, one dead boy and
a tangerine. Customarily the schoolboys
fill the caves with scraps and rinds.
In the center of Hebron, a nest of chewed-
up pips. The women flower the threads

of the piths, but little things want the least
of widows. In the hymns of the turrets,
an order of turtle doves, *Streptopelia turtur*.
Make one dead motion for your father
to the sky and he will forget you.

Thaw

For a sentinel aged particularly, you
dwelled with effortless disinterest,
an Afghani Buddha salvaged from
a wall. You would weigh interminably
upon the egrets. All things in night
-cover. The custom would emerge
inceptively, possibly out toward
an indiscriminate end like a circle
in a field in a dream you would wake
of. How does one cite regret? You,
immaculate industry with a name.
People who stand in their doorways
in winter. People who write about
winter. The empty buildings, the empty
complex at night. When the last wall is not
a wall, who or what will house you?

When We Decided to Build the Wall

I want an olive tree.
I take yours and I smash it.
I move your home sixty
percent to the left, and I take
the lakes. All the fish
are mine. I send the men
to kill your mothers for
the olive trees and your fish,
now my fish. Your men
send their children into
the stems, the ovules
and filaments, the stamens,
pistils, and trees, back
to the source to consume
my children. I scatter
them wildly. In some ways,
one wall can make a factory,
and when the village
works in your factory,
having a god or not having

a god is a matter of profit.
This has a major impact
on how I see flowers and trees.

Matt Mendez
Twitching Heart

Teresa called Chuy at work and asked him to stop by the house and watch the boy. Her call was what he'd wanted, a sign she was cooling off, but Chuy couldn't relax as he sat in his old living room and watched TV. He couldn't take the noise as he flipped through the channels; the yelling of judge and preacher shows used to make him laugh, but now Chuy felt like the dummy defendant getting abused by the judge, the embarrassed pendejo standing next to a preacher in a slick three-piece suit suddenly in need of saving. Teresa had lost her mind over the affair, taking things too far by tossing him out. She was right to be sangrona, he knew, but Chuy also knew his going had nothing to do with another woman. The trouble was Oscar, their eleven-year-old son.

"Put it on cartoons," Oscar said, sitting in front of the television. He'd been talking about some goofy show, one with wizards and dragons and things that would get the boy labeled a total weirdo. Teresa had dressed him in high-water slacks and a button-up she fastened to the top, his head sticking out like a bubble. His boy should be dressed right, looking sharp in a Dallas Cowboy jersey, maybe some Dodger Blue. As a kid Chuy had imagined himself as the Dodger's closer, cutting fastballs to close out big games, and though he'd only once been to the stadium, the green flat-topped grass and plucking organ music filled him up. Now the memories of his family—cooking out on the Fourth of July and lighting Black Cats, dogs howling from the noise and smell of burnt paper—gave him the same full feeling on lonely nights in his apartment.

"Does this mean you're coming back, you being here?" Oscar asked, still watching the television. The boy never looked him in the eye, and Chuy didn't know if he was acting afraid or malcriado.

"Soon," he said. "Your má needs some time, so she says, but yeah, I'll be back. You want that, Oscar? Want your apá home?"

"Yeah," Oscar said, stealing a glance at Chuy.

Chuy thought Oscar was soft because he carried a layer of fat around his waist and face, because he was a crybaby. Teresa tried to convince him that there was nothing wrong with their son; the extra weight would shed away during puberty, and he was sensitive, that's all. She scolded Chuy for forcing Oscar to join Little League even though the boy blew it off, getting stuck in right field and refusing to take his turns at bat, the ball too scary for him. Chuy went to all the games, yelling through the loose chain link fence for Oscar to get in the game and show some heart, but Oscar never did, not like when Chuy pitched the hard and inside stuff to finish off opposing teams in high school. The boy only did what Teresa wanted him to.

"Can you *please* put it on cartoons?"

Chuy switched the television to the all-cartoon channel. A photograph of Teresa and Oscar eating in the park hung on the wall. They smiled from behind the glass. Plastic roses sprouted from vases on the coffee and mismatched end tables, a puffy slipcover on the sofa. The room looked nice, "pretty," and Chuy had to look hard for signs he'd once lived there. Sloppy patches in the drywall, a cigarette burn on the carpet, the ceramic horses he'd bought Teresa on her thirty-first birthday were the only bits left.

"Má said you were supposed to heat up dinner," Oscar said. "I could do it myself, but she doesn't trust me with the oven."

"Your má don't trust no one," Chuy said, remembering the night she booted him. The lines on her face had creased around her eyes and mouth like cracks on a slab of concrete. She'd been pissed, and he'd felt bad for Teresa, her turning old like that.

"*Who* don't I trust?"

Chuy turned and saw Teresa standing in the living room wearing her shapeless blue dress and pointy low-heeled shoes, her old church clothes. Oscar ran to Teresa and wrapped himself around her leg. She eyeballed Chuy. He wore his normal work clothes, a dusty pair of coveralls splattered with paint and plaster, crusted concrete along the bottoms.

"Mamá, I'm hungry," Oscar said. "Apá didn't heat the food."

"Chuy, how could you forget dinner?

"N'hombre, I didn't know what time you were getting back. I'll do it next time."

"Don't be so sure about *next time*."

"I said I was sorry."

"You're always saying sorry. Just do things right for once."

Chuy knew this would turn bad if he kept talking. Teresa had landed a job answering phones for some doctor, probably thought she was big stuff being so independent, but he was glad she'd taken the *jale*. Teresa needed to see how things went outside the house. The world could wear a man down if he hadn't learned to be tougher than the job he was stuck working, but Chuy also needed to prove he could watch Oscar while Teresa learned this. Then maybe she would let him raise Oscar como hombre.

Chuy remembered how fine she used to be—her thin nose barely holding her glasses and slightly crooked teeth that flashed when she smiled. She was once all he wanted, and he couldn't believe how messed up everything had gotten.

"If I moved back, I could watch him better. You know, get back in the flow of things."

"I don't want to talk about it."

"I could sleep on the sofa."

Teresa turned away, and Chuy knew their conversation was over. She had a way of putting an end to things, but their marriage wasn't something she could do that to. She would always be that Catholic girl, for real about forgiveness and second comings.

"Go and get ready," Teresa said to Oscar. "We'll pick up something after we see the new neighbors." Oscar sighed and shuffled to his room.

"What neighbors?" Chuy asked.

"A woman and her daughter."

"No husband, huh?" Chuy wondered if she were making them up.

"Maybe they like it better that way," Teresa said, eyeballing him again.

Chuy wanted to say something but all he did was shrug. He could never talk quick like her, be the first to say something smart. Teresa told him about the new neighbors. They were faith healers from somewhere in California and had moved into the empty Tellez house. The woman's name was María, her daughter, Angélica.

"I could go with you guys, take a look around. Maybe I could help out with some repairs on that old dump, welcome her right." Chuy said, seeing his chance to show Teresa he was trying to be better.

Teresa studied him, her eyes distant headlights. Chuy remembered how fine she used to be—her thin nose barely holding her glasses and slightly crooked teeth that flashed when she smiled. She was once all he wanted, and he couldn't believe how messed up everything had gotten.

"If you want," she finally said.

The old Tellez house wasn't in bad shape, at least not from the outside. Chuy stood on the porch with Teresa and Oscar, the fall evening growing darker from behind the clouds. The swelling heat of the afternoon had slipped away, left the air thin and cold, rainy. Chuy wiped yellow grass and soggy leaves from under his feet. He liked this time of year, things shutting down and taking a break from all the drama.

The house had been abandoned for the past six months, after the Tellez couple died inside—their swamp cooler quit one morning and turned the brick home into an oven, cooked them up. Chuy knew Teresa loved the idea of one day being an old-bird couple like them, but he hated picturing it. On his wedding day, when Padre Maldonado asked if he would take Teresa for as long as he lived, he imagined Teresa looking like her mother, squat and round like a bucket, walking with a limp. That was the last thing he wanted, but he said yes and knew she would give him the son already poking through her wedding dress. Chuy thought he could make things good for the boy, but Oscar didn't do his part.

A woman appeared at the door, a too happy smile on her face. She looked to be in her forties, older than Chuy and Teresa, but dressed younger, sexier. She invited them in like camaradas.

"¡Hola!" María said. "It is nice to see such a good looking family."

María and Teresa hugged. The living room was cluttered with unpacked boxes and trash bags stuffed with clothes. The walls had a fresh coat of pink paint—a shitty splatter job—and was lined with saints: La Virgen de Guadalupe, San Judas, Martín de Porress, Martín de Caballero, Juan Diego, Santo Niño de Atocha. María walked over to Oscar and squeezed his cheeks, her voice squealing as the boy turned red. She reminded Chuy of a telenovela, good in all the bad ways.

María took Chuy's hand and introduced herself, her fingernails glossy and curved, tickling the outside of his palm. Chuy's affair had been with a customer, an old girlfriend who still looked good and promised that he did, too. Chuy shoved his hand in his pocket not wanting Teresa thinking the wrong thing.

"You do handy work," María said. "I can tell a man by his hands."

"Mostly tile," Chuy said. "When I can find the work."

"¡Ay! I must keep you from my kitchen. The floor is bad, and I'll get embarrassed." María touched his shoulder. Chuy was sure all Teresa had heard was *man* and *hands*. His coming had turned out to be a stupid idea. How could he fix things by putting himself in the same trouble as before? He was blowing it.

María led them through the living room with its boxes, the dining room with the puke green carpet, her empty bedroom with all the crosses. Chuy kept his distance from María, staying close to Teresa and the boy, listening as they made small talk. He reminded himself of a stray dog hoping to be taken home. The tour ended in the kitchen and Chuy glanced at the floor. There were gouges in the laminate—some all the way to the slab. Everyone was quiet, and Chuy knew they were waiting for him to say something.

"I thought you had a daughter?" Oscar asked, breaking the silence. "Mamá said she was sick. Did she die?"

"*Cállate*," Chuy said, grabbing Oscar's arm. Teresa sighed, like he was the embarrassing one. Chuy let go. Teresa had never mentioned anything about a sick or dying girl. He wondered what else Teresa had kept from him; what did Oscar know that he didn't? That's the way things always were between those two, them trading secrets all the time.

"It's okay," María said, squatting in front of the boy. "Would you like to meet Angélica? I don't let pilgrims see her this late—she needs her rest, but for you, I'll make the exception." She stood. "For all of you."

Chuy didn't believe in miracles. As a boy he prayed Our Fathers and Hail Mary's all the time, even did Novenas in his bedroom—his má watching to make sure he got the words right, but he never felt what he was supposed to, no swelling in his chest to let him know his dreams would come true. All he got from praying was sore-as-hell knees.

"Say yes if you want to," Teresa said. They stayed in the kitchen, like strangers waiting for the bus, until Oscar finally nodded his head.

María led them to a room at the back of the house. It was dark inside, only the moon lighting the figure beneath a window. The figure was a young girl, her eyes halfway open, stuck someplace between awake and asleep. Chuy felt connected to her, knew exactly where that place was. Angélica's thick black hair spread over her pillow and dropped onto the floor. The room smelled like melting wax, and he felt like he was standing in a church, except he didn't want to leave.

"Is she okay?" Chuy asked, surprised by his own voice.

"The way God wants her to be," María said. "The only way she can do *His* work."

Chuy moved closer, leaving Teresa and Oscar standing with María. Chuy wanted to say something, explain how he was feeling, but Teresa and Oscar wouldn't hear him right. Teresa bowed her head, and Oscar copied her. Chuy thought about his má, a woman who never went a day without praying but still died slowly and without her memory. The girl made Chuy want to believe in miracles.

Oscar had kept quiet after Chuy picked him up, and Chuy decided to give the boy time to get comfortable. It hadn't been easy to get Teresa to go along with bringing the boy—he'd promised to keep close, take breaks and not let Oscar saw anything. Teresa always worried about Oscar getting hurt, spending too much time on things that wouldn't put him in college. That's our job as parents, she'd always tell him. The boy needed to know that life wasn't in books. Life got made with strong hands, and only a father could teach that.

Chuy drove through his old neighborhood, past Our Lady of Guadalupe and the Hilltop Barbershop where Old Tony still gave haircuts for seven bucks. He loved the place, especially in the early morning when nobody was around to see the night thin and the sun over the mountains. He pulled up at María's and looked over at Oscar; he was asleep, his eyes pinched shut. It had taken Oscar twenty-two months to learn how to walk but only four to say mamá. Teresa had been so proud, telling Chuy how smart the boy was, gifted. Chuy left Oscar inside the truck, walked to the house and rang the bell.

"I didn't think you'd be here so early," María said, opening the door. "We're not ready." María didn't look glamorous this time, the skin on her face tugging down like sheets on a clothesline. He wondered if he'd woken up Angélica, if that were something she could do. He remembered her arms knotted above her chest like mesquite branches, her frozen face. She'd freaked him out, but he wanted to see her again, found himself thinking about cancers being cured, old ladies in wheelchairs standing and walking around, money found buried in backyards.

"I only got one day with my helper," Chuy said, nodding his head at Oscar. "Gotta finish everything today."

"Entonces," María said, opening the door. "It's good to see a boy learning from his father. That is the most important thing."

Chuy and Oscar cleared the kitchen and scrubbed the linoleum with soapy water. When the floor dried Chuy handed Oscar the end of a chalk line and stretched it across the length of the room. A plume of blue dust puffed in the air as he snapped it against the laminate. Oscar surprised Chuy by moving when he did, figuring out where he needed to be and looking for what to do next. "Now the real work starts," Chuy said, cutting open a box of tiles leftover from a job he'd done on the Westside, some gringo's rec-room that had pictures of his sons hanging on the walls. They smiled in their Coronado T-Bird uniforms and held trophies with little brass baseball dudes on them—trophies lined the wall, too. Chuy remembered thinking how that gringo had it all: money, a good house, a pair of sons who would do him right.

Chuy handed Oscar a tile. "First, you have to check each one for cracks before you set it. Even a small one will bust it apart when the thinset dries." Oscar nodded, and

Chuy wondered if he should explain what thinset did, how it hardened and turned little cracks into big ones, but Oscar seemed to understand as much as he needed to.

The sun came up and Chuy stopped to watch the orange light cut through the window. The house didn't have the same hopeful feeling it had had before. This felt like just another job, and he wondered what the hell he'd been thinking. Miracles. How stupid could he be? Oscar sat and checked the tiles for cracks, a pile of empty boxes behind him and a stack of good tiles in front. Chuy never actually checked them. He liked to work fast and most of the time spotted a bad one before setting it—though he sometimes missed and had to fix the mess afterward, but Oscar seemed happy, like he was playing one of his weird games, so Chuy left him to it.

Chuy went to the porch and poured the thinset into a bucket. His knees and back hurt like always, and Chuy felt glad that Oscar was smart and would never have to work like this. But it was the kind of glad that turned rotten by thinking about it; part of him wanted Oscar to end up at a job like his, to show Teresa that nobody's dreams are better because nobody's come true. Chuy added water from the hose and mixed everything until it was thick like peanut butter, lugged it back to the kitchen where he found Oscar standing over the sink.

"It was an accident," Oscar said, pouring water on his hand. "One of the tiles was broken."

"I told you to be careful," Chuy said. Chuy dropped the bucket and grabbed Oscar's hand. A busted tile had gashed him across the palm, and Chuy pressed hard and waited to see if the blood would thin. He heard Teresa's voice in his head: *I can't trust you por nada. One day and you cut his hand off.*

Oscar stared at his hand and whimpered.

"Don't cry," Chuy said while squeezing, the thin bones poking against his fingers. "Don't make it worse."

"I'm not."

Chuy opened Oscar's hand to see how deep the cut went, and Oscar cried. Chuy thought of hugging the boy the way Teresa did when he was hurt, but he kept squeezing, knowing it wouldn't stop the blood from coming.

"What's wrong, Oscarcito?" María asked, rushing into the room. She wrapped her arms around the boy.

"I wasn't messing around. I promise," Oscar said between chokes of air.

"Of course you weren't," María said. She calmed Oscar, and Chuy was both jealous and relieved. He'd wanted to tell Oscar that everyone got hurt on the job; his hand would scar and that scar would stay with him forever. It was something he could look back on and remember, better than a picture because mistakes were real. María went to the cupboard and grabbed a bag of flour, dropped a lump in Oscar's palm and watched as it globbed into a reddish ball.

"Make a fist and hold it tight," she said and wrapped his hand in a kitchen towel. "Let me get some orange peels for you to chew on, to stop the bleeding." María disappeared into the dining room.

"Here," Chuy said wrapping the towel tighter around Oscar's fist. "Do you want to call má? I won't get mad."

"No," he said, turning away. "I want to stay with you and finish the job. I don't want you to go again." Teresa would blame Chuy for the hand, say he never looked out for their son. She always told Chuy how Oscar deserved the chance for a better life—the chance they never got, but Chuy knew what Teresa really meant: *He deserved better than you.*

Chuy wrapped Oscar's hand with a roll of electrical tape he found at the bottom of his tool bag, going over the kitchen towel until Oscar's hand looked like a black flipper. Teresa would eventually stop by to check on Chuy, overreact and take Oscar away when she saw the hand—probably for good this time. Chuy had flunked her little test and felt bad for thinking about it that way—him losing, them winning, everything fading like old paint.

Chuy crouched on the floor and spread a glob of thinset with the notched end of his trowel, making even rows across the linoleum. He set the first tile and pressed down, collapsing pockets of air in the thick adhesive. Oscar sat beside him, passing tiles with his good hand and chewing orange peels. María had gone, saying she needed to get Angélica ready for visitors. The house was quiet, and Chuy wondered how Angélica got ready or helped pilgrims. She was barely alive.

Oscar passed another tile without saying a word. The boy sat still, and for the first time Chuy recognized himself in his son. He had the same slightly open mouth and hard eyes he recognized from the mirror. When Oscar was a baby he'd cried all the time—his lungs like balloons filled with air and then deflating in long shrieks, but that noise had given Chuy hope for the future. Maybe the boy would be one of those marathon runners, gliding across giant cities and never losing a breath. Chuy had wanted Oscar to be an athlete, a *vato* who had people looking up to him. A man with respect.

Chuy and Oscar stopped for a break and sat in the living room eating tortillas con jámon. It was noon and the tiles were setting, a few more cuts and they'd be done.

Father and son had worked all morning and mostly without talking. Chuy could tell Oscar was nervous about saying the wrong thing, about asking him why he'd gone away and if he was ever coming back. Chuy would have tried to answer, but he didn't *know* why, at least not the kind of why that would make sense.

The woman's name was Yvette, and Chuy had known her from high school. She was still fine, but that's not why Chuy did what he did. Things between him and Teresa were *chingada*, and in a way Oscar had made them that way—their fighting for who the boy should be was never ending. With Yvette, Chuy had wanted another chance, another son. He pictured this boy playing in the park, not thinking about colleges and futures, about all the dumb things he could do to mess his life up. Yvette called Teresa when she'd found out Chuy was married and told her everything.

A car pulled into the driveway, a brown tin can with bubbled tint and smoky exhaust. A man and woman climbed out, some old timers Chuy didn't recognize. They walked with a boy. He was too skinny to be healthy, his shoulders popping out from under his ashy skin, his head swiveling on his neck. Oscar had always been healthy, so healthy Chuy had never noticed. Chuy went to the porch.

"¿Es la casa de Angélica?" The woman asked, her voice tired. The man, who looked even older up close, his hair like the white wisps of a viejo cactus, kept his head down.

"Está adentro, señora," Chuy answered and held the door. He could tell this was the last chance for them, that they'd tried it all and were ready to leave their hopes to María and the miracle girl. Oscar stood up when María appeared from Angélica's room, like he knew something was about to happen—Oscar had always been good at that. María met the family at the door and was glamorous all over again.

"Ayúdeme con él," the man said to Chuy. Chuy went over to the boy, leaving Oscar alone. Chuy cradled the sick boy in his arms, and even though he was older than Oscar—his eyes yellow and his skin both thin and rough like tamale husks—he weighed nothing. Chuy felt responsible for him, like holding on would keep them both from floating away. Oscar eyeballed Chuy—giving him that Teresa look—and he realized he hadn't held Oscar since he was a baby. Chuy wondered if there was something broken inside of him, something wrong with the way he loved. Chuy reached down and tried to grab Oscar's hand, but he pulled away, hiding the taped mess behind his back.

María led everyone to Angélica's room and told them her story. Angélica had been swimming at a city pool when she slipped and hit her head, drowned in front of everybody. At the hospital Angélica was put on machines, and doctors told María her daughter would die as soon as they were turned off. So María prayed for a miracle—Ave Marías, Novenas, everything she could think of—and when the hospital decided to shut her down, because it was too expensive and too late anyways, Angélica kept breathing, living.

María took her to church that day, right to the altar where a Mass was going and a priest giving Communion. She demanded he give to Angélica, one body to help the other, but before the *cura* put the wafer in the frozen girl's mouth, it transformed. The Host softened into a miniature beating heart, a ring of thorns gashing the sides, and it burst as soon as it touched the surface of Angélica's dry tongue. From then on María said she could see the Holy Spirit glowing in her daughter's eyes. Angélica had cured the priest's diabetes, or so María had said.

María went on to explain the rules. They could pray and ask Angélica to speak to God. They could light candles and touch her, but only on the arms. No pictures. Donations at the end. Chuy imagined the sick boy touching Angélica and then coming to life, like a dry sponge soaking up water. Maybe that's how it worked, Angélica's body sucking tumors and bad blood and bad hearts and trading it with the life she couldn't use. Chuy hoped Oscar would touch her, and if not he'd put the sick boy down and make him. Angélica could fix his hand. Fix everything.

The room looked different than it had that first night. The moonlight had been replaced by the sun, making the room hot and real. Ceramic statues of San Judas and La Virgen de Guadalupe were in the corners of the room. Prayer candles of every kind of saint—San Cayetano, Agustín, Pascual Bailón, Lorenzo, and Santa Bárbara—flickered. Angélica lay in the middle of the room, wearing a pink dress with lacy trim. She breathed with the help of a machine, made a slow sucking noise. A purple blanket with small metal hearts and prayer cards, with fading photographs of sick nanas and tatas and niños at hospitals, of families smiling—memories of the good times— and little kid drawings with blue skies and frowning faces were pinned to it and pulled to her waist. The doorbell rang.

Chuy carried the sick boy closer to Angélica. Oscar stayed back. The old man motioned for Chuy to put his son down, and he did, though he'd wanted to hold on longer. Chuy wanted to be part of any miracle Angélica could make. Chuy watched as the mother placed her son's bony hand inside the miracle girl's, could hear Teresa calling for Oscar from the front door. The mother of the sick boy cried, the corners of her mouth lined with spit. María lit incense and made the air thick and cloudy, a bad dream about to end. Chuy knew Teresa would eventually let herself in the house.

María sprinkled the sick boy with holy water and huddled everyone around Angélica. Chuy grabbed Oscar and took him to her, deciding he needed something to hope for, too. They stood next to the sick boy, and Chuy took Oscar's taped hand and placed it on the miracle girl. A layer of black hair covered Angélica's cheeks and above her lip. An oily patch of acne around her nose. Chuy felt pinche for noticing, for butting in, for letting things get bad enough for miracles in the first place.

"Pray," Chuy said to Oscar but more to himself. Chuy hadn't prayed in years, thought asking for help never worked, but as he closed his eyes and squeezed Oscar's hand, he surprised himself. He asked for whoever was listening to make things right for the boy—for Oscar to be what he was supposed to and not anything else. Chuy opened his eyes and turned around, saw Teresa in the doorway.

"Oscar," Teresa said, waving him over.

"Má," Oscar said, suddenly breaking from Chuy and running toward her. Chuy backed away from Angélica. The family hadn't noticed them, like they were all frozen in some terrible moment: the sick boy's parents with heavy heads, María's clenched face, the sick boy and Angélica lost.

Teresa looked over Oscar's hand on the porch. They were out of place by the scraps of tile and empty bags of thinset and grout, the tossed around tools. Teresa peeled off the tape. The kitchen towel was soaked with blood, and the adhesive left a grayish gum on the outside of Oscar's wrist. His hand was still clenched in a fist.

"What happened?" Teresa asked.

"It was my fault," Chuy said, meeting them outside. "A tile cut him when I wasn't looking." Oscar tried to hide the hand, but Teresa grabbed it.

"Look at his hand, Chuy." Drops of blood fell to the ground. "Ábrate la mano, Oscar." Oscar didn't move, and Teresa pulled his fingers open. Clumps of red flour caked the rim of his wound, fresh blood in the middle. It ran down Oscar's arm as Teresa lifted it to show Chuy. It looked worse than before. How could he not have known how bad the injury was, that the boy needed to be looked out for? "This needs a doctor, Chuy. Why didn't you call me?"

"I told him to tough it out," Chuy lied. "That we had a job to finish." Chuy didn't want Teresa to know Oscar had wanted to stay, to have her feel like she needed to keep fighting. Chuy knew Teresa would give the boy what he couldn't, would do the things that had always been hard for him.

Chuy thought of Angélica, of the small twitching heart pulsing and flexing on the surface of the miracle girl's cracked tongue. Her body would keep living, spreading until her pink dress got too small and she became a burden to anyone who loved her. Chuy didn't know if Angélica had ever cured cancer or anything else. Her life was a silent and stuck way to be. A life Chuy knew.

"I can't believe you," Teresa said, rewrapping Oscar's hand.

Teresa picked up their son. He was too big for her, but she lugged him to her car, his feet dragging on the ground as he slipped from her arms. Teresa belted Oscar in the back seat, looked ahead as she cranked the engine and drove off. Oscar turned to watch his father, and Chuy, knowing better than to turn away, waved goodbye.

John Lindgren
Polish Folklore

There is an old folk saying told to children on winter nights, told at the black hour, when the she-wolf with her cubs claws at the door, and a bottle of vodka squatting on the oak table beside a candle flame strangles in a noose of smoke, that one must never walk backwards. Only the dead walk backwards, as do our shadows. They walk backwards into the future with eyes forever fixed upon the past. And so, to walk backwards is to imitate their ways. Our shadows do not walk backwards, of course, but at times they walk behind us, before us, or at our sides, filled with the color of grief and misfortune, like hats, gloves and umbrellas the forgetful leave on trains. They have no mouths but would love for us to acknowledge them; no lips, but would love a simple kiss. They have no hands to speak of, but would love to place one tenderly on our shoulder. All are victims of loss, loneliness and endless despair.

Each night they swim or fly off on a rendezvous with the dead, to converse, or to receive instructions. If you wake from a sleep speaking a language you no longer remember, and glass sentences lie glistening on the floor, they are like small tongues you've just swallowed, little fish swimming among the sapphire coral of the bones, knocking now and then, and listening at the walls of the skin. Or small birds darting among the ruby thickets of the blood, alighting the moment you fall back to sleep, to resume their songs.

If you write with the ink of a firefly on your shadow by day, you are sending messages to the other world. And at night, dazzled by the scrawl of so many lightning bugs weaving among the dark trees, it is the other world writing back.

When we walk in the sun our shadows are barges of moonlight. But there is a certain time of day when our shadow's length equals our own, and it becomes clear and transparent as a pool of newlyfallen rain. And as much as you wish to cup your hands like the moon's chalice and dip them in that purest water to slake an inexplicable thirst, you must not, for surely you will die.

If Death casts a shadow, it is only the image of our lives in a mirror, a place where right is left, up is down, where the lies we tell our friends are identical to the lies we tell ourselves to live. So a shot of vodka friends! Who knows what stories are being spun in the spindles in the grain on a wooden table? Who knows how long it will snow, or if this night will ever end?

Na zdrowie all! A shot for the she-wolf, a draft for each of her cubs, and another for the man in the black cloak wielding the moon as a scythe. And a last one, to the miraculous, the terrible beauty and strangeness of it all. How mysterious that any of us should be here, any of us at all?

Cole Swensen and David St. John, editors
American Hybrid: A Norton Anthology of New Poetry

Reviewed by Renée Ashley

Did you know that a rutabaga is a hybrid, a cross between a turnip and cabbage? Did you know this crossbreeding is not the product of modern gene-splicing, but took place naturally sometime in the Middle Ages? The American Institute of Cancer Research (AICR) eNews of August 2007 says the rutabaga "contains qualities of both its parents, firmer than a turnip with a stronger flavor," and states, as well, that "[p]retty much all produce sold today are hybrids, but typical hybrids are crosses within the same type of fruit or vegetable." I didn't know that about the produce— though I probably should have. But have you been to an upscale market lately? Have you seen the more obvious and fittingly-named manifestations? Pluots (plum + apricot, about seventy-five percent plum)? Apriums (apricot + plum, about seventy-five percent apricot)? Have you come across nectaplums or peacharines? Nectacotums? Peacotums? How about broccoflower or broccolini? They're out there.

It seems that, in just about any venue, a great many of the most interesting and viable things happen when the elements are mixed. For instance, all my dogs have been found-or-pound mongrels—and I've never had a bad or sickly dog. In fact, I'm a mixed breed myself: French, Spanish, Welsh somewhere along the line, and who knows what else, and I'm a relatively healthy specimen, considering—and though I look more like my mother than my father, I have his disposition and eyes. A Mai Tai is a mixed drink, you know, and the glorious Margarita. Much of the food we eat is

W.W. Norton & Co.: New York, NY, 2009.

made by combining ingredients: a fine seafood paella doesn't come into the world fully formed. Even my best attempt at swimming falls somewhere between a breast stroke, a dog paddle, and a slow sinking. We take a little of this and a little of that and we make it our own.

Without even thinking about it we have become ready users of the vocabulary associated with hybridization: *assimilation, incorporation, synthesis, fusion, amalgamation—minglement*, to use a word we've lost but should find again. Whatever you want to call it, it's here. It's been here. And the astute editors of *American Hybrid: A Norton Anthology of New Poetry* have given us a volume to stand on while the word is spread and codified. It's a fine step in acknowledging the protean state of contemporary poetry, in moving to the foreground what Keith Waldrop could easily have been speaking of at the end of his poem, "First Draw the Sea," when he said, equal signs included:

> =
> *. . . this corner turned.*
>
> =
> Unattended ground.

We are categorists both at heart and out of necessity. Categories keep the world that comes at us in such rush and abundance—and from so many varied sources—manageable. And while I am neither a connoisseur of nor a lobbyist for categories (for the most part, I'm sure, determinations such as categories at best oversimplify and at worst mislead or even falsify), I also understand they're a necessary and expedient shorthand. But in the case of *hybrid*, as in *American Hybrid: A Norton Anthology of New Poetry*, it is, though admittedly vast and open-ended, spot on. The dichotomous *traditional* and *experimental* categories no longer cover the range of possibilities (if they ever did). *Hybrid* is a category that is utterly apt and filled with possible and promising permutations. It's also a signal that a poetry reader's arena of expectation must be wide open and poised for change. This is a good thing in both poetry and life. It strengthens both the figurative and literal gene pools.

Cole Swensen points out in her introduction:

> While the new is an important common denominator of much hybrid work, it is a combinatory new, one that recognizes that "there is nothing new under the sun" and embraces the postmodern understanding of the importance of connection: that given elements are often less crucial than the relationships between them.

Ann Lauterbach's poem "After Mahler" is an excellent example of that "combinatory new." Within its confines it acts out its own evolutionary combinations—its combinations within its combinations. The first stanza consists of six end-stopped lines of syntactically-correct sentences.

> A thousand minutes came out of the tottering state.
> The bed of thyme moved within its bearings like a dream.
> He answered, *tomorrow*.
> Someone else was screaming on the radio; people laughed.
> The cat has been dead for some time now.
> The wedding party's bright joy looked strange from the streaking jet.

But something has knocked that "correct" status awry, and we find things just slightly strange. In the first line, "minutes" come out of the "state"—*what*? Okay, we might think, we can work with that, it's a metaphor. But then the second line is slightly less intelligible: an herb bed is moving "within its bearings." The third line begins with a pronoun that has no referent. The fourth is plausible, but what does it have to do with the lines that come before? Who is that "screaming on the radio"? Someone *else*? Other than whom? The speaker? The *he* of the previous line? The fifth line, the one about the dead cat, comes out of nowhere as well—what cat? It's *the* cat, not *a* cat, but we haven't heard anything about a cat! And the sixth line's perspective is that of someone "streaking" away on a jet. The speaker? The *he*? The cat? The people on the radio? No clue. Within a normative syntax there are content entries of lines with separate focuses and without transitions. The usually smooth road is a tad rocky and the reader's footing is unsure; she is knocked off balance more than once. *Combinatory*. Excellent word. It explains so much.

Our human drive toward commingling—for whatever reason: nature, nurture, convenience, or the will of some capricious god—is a strong one. And I imagine that by now we're hard put to find purity in either line or lineage. For many of us, the hybrid personality is part of the human package.

One example: at a time when it was uncommon, my mother had her first and only child at thirty-nine. Ma dressed "like a lady" and acted the lady until it suited her to do otherwise, until, as in the development of a poem, the traditional expression available to her let her down, and her own nature—nature and perceived necessity—pushed her into a mode of discourse that forced the observer to adjust his idea of how a woman dressed "like a lady" was free to act. Ma tells me strangers stopped her almost daily to comment on her adorable "granddaughter." It hurt her feelings and damaged her vanity; it pissed her off. But she set them straight, she assured me, in no uncertain terms. It was simple: she stood very straight, turned her smiling face toward their own, and said in a tone that could have stripped the enamel right off their teeth, "She's my daughter, *asshole*." She'd be tugging on her gloves as she said it.

There always were—and still are, I might add, and she's ninety-eight now—disparities between Ma's appearance and her actions that manifested even without unintentional baiting from total strangers. I didn't understand this until later. I was a child then—what did I know? My mother was the whole world. I knew nothing about adults other than her, my gentle and absent father, and my teachers who were, without exception, singular paragons of virtue. Really. They were. So as far as I knew, there were three camps of adults: teachers, kind and absent fathers, and Ma. I never questioned that they were different. Ma believed with absolute certainty—and still may, if you ask her, though she's dispensed with the gloves and traded the straight skirt and pumps for a purple sweatsuit and Velcro-closured walking shoes—that if you wore white gloves, if you kept your knees together and dressed like a lady, you could get away with just about anything.

Let me tell you a story, another true one.

It had to be around 1960, so Ma was about fifty and I was probably ten-ish. My mother still worked the PBX board in the rotunda of the old San Mateo County Courthouse. It was the kind of old-fashioned telephone exchange that had long cords—gray with red bits woven through—that pulled up from a table console and had brass plugs at the end. Seated, Ma, along with two other women, would pull those plugs up and shove them into a low wall of small, brass-rimmed holes that rose from the console and were marked with extension numbers. The call was the plug; the hole was the destination. The match made the connection.

Some of the details of this particular day are hazy, some are as clear as clean glass. I don't know why I'm at my mother's workplace. And I don't know why we're in the elevator, since, if she had been working, we could have gone right out the big glass brass-trimmed doors that led from the rotunda out to the wide concrete steps down to Main Street. But I see Ma with her ever-so-slightly-greenish, brown-tinted hair wearing a yellow dress (which has a black pattern on it that looks suspiciously like the pattern on the wallpaper in our stairway at home). The skirt of the dress is slim, the bodice cap-sleeved. The wide neckline has a split, rolled collar that buttons with one large black button on the left. Her waist is belted with a thin black patent-leather belt. Her shoes and bag match her belt. I don't even have to imagine that part to know it's true. Her handbag is slipped over her left arm, and her wrist-length white gloves are gathered in her right hand.

The elevator doors slide open and a young man in a gray suit holds the door back with his hand so it won't close on us. We enter one at a time, Ma first, and we turn to face the front. The doors close. I am to the right and slightly behind my mother, who stands center-car. The young man is to her left and just behind her. She smiles a warm "Thank you" after he asks for and pushes the button for our floor.

I am sneaking peeks at him behind my mother's back. He can't see me, I'm certain, and, when he does turn his head in my direction, I drop my gaze to the floor. It is the first time I remember looking at someone or something and having a perception that did not somehow include my mother. Evidently, it was my inkling: that instant when I first realized that a young man (or an old boy) might be . . . interesting. Nobody speaks. The old elevator makes its aged complaint in the silence around us. My mother takes her compact out of her purse and pats at her nose with the puff, then at that indented space between her lower lip and chin. She checks the mirror, snaps the compact shut, and drops it back in her bag. The small wooden-walled box we are riding in gives its customary jostle and is just about to settle at its destination floor when my mother farts. Not a ladylike fluff. Not a surprise-us-all toot. Or a poot. Or a whistle or a pop. Not a sound that could be mistaken for anything but what it is: a cheek-slapping, moist and slippery horn blast that goes on and on until it finally loses steam, whimpers and dies wetly out. There occurs one of those moments of stunned silence that we all have experienced when nobody has even begun to think yet. The elevator doors open and my mother, head erect, eyes straight ahead, strides out of the car and into the granite-floored lobby, pulling her white gloves over her fingers and snapping them down onto her palms brusquely, as if nothing at all has transpired. There's another pause—a nanosecond, probably—before she notices that I am not beside her. She spins around with an annoyed look on her freshly-powdered face. I'm in the elevator and I can't move. The young man is holding the door for me, the door repeatedly bumping against his hand in an effort to fulfill its repetitive destiny and close. His lips are taut and trembling. I already know what's going to happen and there's nothing I can do to stop it. She says my name: "Ruh-uh-*nay*!" She looks at me in disgust while she draws out and wavers that schwa of the first syllable and snaps the second as though it is a third glove to be yanked into place. There's a marked crescendo at the end. She repeats the name with a different emphasis: "Ruh-*na-aaay*," she says this time, drawing out the second syllable in a melisma of utter horror. Her arms drop to her sides, her bag to her hand. Then she says it: "Have a little *couth*, Renée. Say *excuse me* to the man and come along." She turns and takes a few steps on the polished floor, moving toward the bank of glass doors.

For the first time in my life, I do not know where my allegiance lies. With my mother? Or with my own, new perception of the possibility of something of importance outside of her? The balance, of course, topples in an instant; I can't look at the young man, nor do I say *excuse me*, but I do come along. I walk blindly in a straight line toward my mother, who is walking toward one of the doors trimmed in brass with horizontal brass releases. She pushes the bar and holds the door open. I walk out behind her. As far as I can remember, the incident is never addressed again until I'm an adult, when she denies it ever happened. The funny thing, though, is that even in my alarm, even in the at-that-point most humiliating moment of my life, I can see that it is funny. I'd been living, say a decade or so, with my mother's sense of humor, and my mother is a funny woman. But it was also the beginning of other-consciousness. A bit of differentiation. The world got bigger. Minglement happened. Both my mother and I were manifestations of minglement right then. Ma was "a lady" who farted in elevators and blamed her daughter, not a traditional category, and I had one foot in the child world and one in that of adolescence, a place that harbors humiliation in cartloads. We were singular hybrids, each our own, at that moment.

Humans operate on multiple, complex levels. We don't have binary minds. Our actions and their degrees of effectiveness and/or appearance exist on multiple continuums—imaginary, yes, but conceptually pretty sound. Beyond over-simplification there is the gray area, all those mixed impulses, those aggregate, sometimes conflicting presentations and articulations, those effects that are the amalgam *minglement*. The strengths of nature and nurture and accident. The ones that move us forward. The most interesting to interact with.

And in poetry, human endeavor that it is, I see the continuum of possibility this way: three animals, none human, in full-body profile, nose—so to speak—to tail. First, at the far left, an indigo bunting (bird: approximately five inches in length; seven-to-nine inch wingspan; weighing approximately half an ounce; male, in breeding plumage; brilliant blue). Then, in the center, a smallish African elephant (mammal: height at shoulder, ten feet; weight, about eleven thousand pounds; gray). And lastly, far right, a ruby-throated hummingbird (bird: approximately three to four inches in length; three to four inches in wingspan; weighing from less than one-tenth to less than a quarter of an ounce). The bright blue bunting is traditional verse; the elephant is the bulk of what we know, the gray area of hybrid poems and spin-offs; and the hummingbird, with its fiery green and iridescent red, is the radically experimental end of the continuum. And even then, within *American Hybrid*, fractal-like within the elephant itself, we have fuzzy-edged representatives of the same three designations: Reginald Shepherd's stunning poem, "Direction of Fall," might fall to the traditional/lyric end of the hybridic spectrum ("And then this ruined sky again. Memory / came like migratory birds calling *reaper, reaper, / reaper*, hungry ghosts threshing distance // at the extremity of private sound . . .). And then there's Stacy Doris's excerpt from "Cheerleader's Guide to the World: Council Book," which leaps out of the verbal, periodically, into the iconographic to include her irreproducible (at least here) *x, o,* line, and arrow diagrams of various cheerleading moves, and then back again to verbal moves such as this one that follows immediately upon a diagram and breaks with only visual warning, once again, into another, a different diagram.

> This is about Our Country and Our Culture
> since even before they were Ours.
> That's why it sandwiches Popol Vuh Paterson Tibetan Dead Jigme Lingpa Pindar
> Rah rah:"

Surely this might be a move toward what could be considered the experimental.

Of course, as Swensen says in her introduction, "[H]ybridity is . . . in itself no guarantee of excellence, and the decentralizing influences . . . make it harder to achieve consensus or even to maintain stable critical criteria; instead, these factors put more responsibility on individual readers to make their own assessments, which can in turn create stronger readers in that they must become more aware of and refine their own criteria." The burden, then, falls to the reader, fairly enough, to make out what she sees—hence the expedience and genuine helpfulness of the categories.

Swensen gives, as well, a superb overview of the perceived historical poetic bipartisanism, and it *is* interesting, an intelligent and concise overview of poetry and its schools and schisms. The anthology contains more than seventy poets, and several pieces by each poet, each set prefaced by a short introduction by the editors: an insightful paragraph on how to approach the work and narrow the category by technique and/or effect, and a paragraph of biography.

Swensen and St. John considered for inclusion only poets who, at the time they began reading for the anthology, had already published a minimum of three volumes and so we have examples from familiar names such as John Ashbery, Albert Goldbarth, Jorie Graham, Lyn Hejinian, Brenda Hillman, Fanny Howe, Alice Notley, Keith and Rosmarie Waldrop, and Marjorie Welish, along with others both equally and less well-known. St. John points out that, ironically, their criteria for inclusion "excluded many of those younger poets whose work [they'd] first looked to as models of hybridization." He adds, "their anthology is yet to come." I look forward to this addition with both glee and impatience.

But *American Hybrid* as it stands is a sturdy, fascinating, and useful volume, a foundational collection, that I have, reading more deeply, fallen in love with. It's a desert island book. Included is work by poets I was already acquainted with as well as work from a few poets who were brand new to me. I rediscovered poets I recalled, mistakenly, as being landlocked in airtight categories, for instance the marvelous poet James Galvin, who I had earlier pegged as tightly mainstream and who I found now "exploding his modes of making sense" and ". . . leaving the relationships among his lines and phrases ever more open-ended." Approaches run the gamut within the anthology from the edgy minimalism of Rae Armantrout to Mei-Mei Berssenbrugge's arty, maximal lines (which were so long the editors had them printed landscape-style on the page). I found non sequiturs, visible cross-outs, play (as in *theater*) formatting, integrated photographs, variations on the use of white space, of typography, of line lengths, punctuations, stanza formats, dividing symbols, and disruptions of syntax and meaning. Marvelous lexical tip-offs in the poet introductions gave me articulations to hold onto while I read the pages that followed: *indeterminancy, abstract lyricism, fractured sensibilities, philosophical speculation, loose referentiality, unstable pronouns.* This is happy-making, freeing language, and intelligent reading and observation.

And it is proof, as well, that our poetry has taken a deluxe turn toward what can happen naturally; that, as Michael Burkard writes here, "We don't have to make a sentence if we don't want to." "

Our poetry," says St. John, "should be as various as the natural world, as rich and peculiar in its potential articulations." He is, he says, ". . . persuaded by the idea of an American poetry based on plurality, not purity." Me, too.

Like language itself, the nature of poetic output has become fluid, unfixed. We are writing, now, poems that feel their way—or seem to feel their way—through the writer, from experience; through imagination and association, rather than through the predetermined form. We borrow from, expand upon, react to—combining in some way, shape or form—all the time. We *are* what we take in and process directly or indirectly: a little nature, a little nurture, a whim, an impulse, a cogent plan. "Like species," Forest Gander writes, "poems are not invented, but develop out of a kind of discourse, each poet tensed against another's poetics, in conversation . . ."

"[E]verything is relational," says Mei-Mei Berssenbrugge. Our artistic receptors function under the pressure of what we know or suspect. We are the gray area personified, and it's a fine thing that the poem, as human endeavor, has been recognized, or as Swenson writes it, to be ". . . increasing the expressive potential of language itself—while also remaining committed to the emotional spectra of lived experience."

The newsletter quoted at the beginning of this essay puts it beautifully ". . . move over apples and bananas . . ." it said. Move over dichotomy of *traditional* and *experi-*

mental. Blatantly or subtly, we've got mongrel fruit. And surprises. The skirts of poetic convention are being lifted and they're flashing a new bit of intelligence and éclat. We need to broaden our language in order to keep up. *American Hybrid: A Norton Anthology of New Poetry* is here to help us do that.

Alan Gilbert
Interview with Robert Polito

As Director of the Writing Program at The New School in Manhattan, Robert Polito frequently conducts public discussions with various invited writers and scholars. I've attended a number of these over the years, though I've never seen Polito himself interviewed. Thus, I was excited to receive an invitation from *The Literary Review* to sit in the seat Polito usually occupies and move his work into the spotlight.

Given Polito's expansive range of knowledge and interests, it's fitting that I met with him on an afternoon in late March when he was shuttling between Italy, the Hudson Valley, and Chicago. The interview took place over lunch in lower Manhattan, and focused on his powerful new book of poems, *Hollywood & God*. But, again, given Polito's polymathic inclinations, the conversation covered a host of topics, ending with his thoughts on how the concept of "Manifest Destiny" might function in the year 2009.

ALAN GILBERT: Your new book, *Hollywood & God*, has a striking title that succinctly captures much of the glamour, sordidness and heretical quality to the work. It also sums up your broad range of interests—from film noir to the prosody of the King James Bible. Can you talk a little bit about the title?
ROBERT POLITO: The working title of the book actually was "Deep Deuce," also the title of one of the poems. I first heard about "Deep Deuce" as the shorthand name for a street in Oklahoma City I visited in connection with my Jim Thompson biography years ago. It was the old jazz street; the phrase means, "way down on Second Street."

Robert Polito, *Hollywood & God*, The University of Chicago Press: Chicago, IL, 2009.

By the time I saw "Deep Deuce" there was nothing much left beyond a few foundations, walls, and facades. Second Street and everything around had been destroyed during some mad imposition of urban renewal with the intention of course of building it back up—but there would never be enough money. You can read about "Deep Deuce" in Ralph Ellison's novels and letters.

When I talked to my friends about the book of poems I was writing, I routinely referred to it not as "Deep Deuce," but "Hollywood and God," though never then thinking I could get away with that as a title. So, I already knew those really are the polarities, if that's the right word for them—the polarities and something like the intersections I was exploring in the poems. I eventually realized "Hollywood and God" was a much more focused and concise title for the materials of these poems than "Deep Deuce," which additionally would have required I explain it every time I said it aloud. The book tracks a continuum between what might be regarded as transcendence and what we call celebrity culture. But I really stumbled on that title; didn't realize right away just how perfect a description it was for what I was doing, and possibly for certain iconic contemporary as well as historical trends and impulses in our life.

Because of my Jim Thompson biography, *Savage Art,* I'm associated with noir, but I came to noir late, really, through Thompson, who I discovered only in the early 1980s. I instantly loved what in noir recalls so many other not obviously noir books I love—like Samuel Beckett, Melville, Hawthorne, Dickinson or Flaubert. In many ways, I come to noir through Beckett, and I think of noir as these beautiful sentences telling you the most terrible things. The comedy in Thompson also struck me as close to the comedy in Beckett, or even in Celine.

I sense a tremendous elegance and wit in Thompson, and also a darkness, and even occasional savagery, in some of James Merrill's work . . . in *The Changing Light of Sandover*, provoked largely by fears of nuclear annihilation and environmental ruin. The relationship between the living and the dead always fascinated me, how could it not? And that's both noirish and the essence of poetry. I think of poetry as a conversation between us and the dead, the great poets out of the past.

AG: On a panel at The New School last year titled "Mixing Genres," you spoke about your love for writing that blurs the distinctions between poetry, fiction and essay. Your new book, *Hollywood & God*, combines poetry, fiction and non-fictional elements. Did you consciously set out to write a mixed-genre work?
RP: No, not consciously, at least not at the outset. I didn't know the form of this book until I was well into it. It took a long time to discover the form. I was telling myself I

was going to write a book-length poem about something I called Elvis Presley's America, whatever that meant, and there are still echoes of that original scheme in this book. I also realized some of the essays I was writing, or wished to write, were circling the same materials I wanted to pursue in the poems. The three essays run along a continuum of autobiographical accuracy, and my hope is that there is an autobiographical continuity in the tone. Robert Lowell and Elizabeth Bishop, of course, imported prose into books of poems. But, as I said at The New School that night, I think not only is there a tendency in the most exciting books of the last fifteen years to mix genre all but unclassifiably—I was thinking of Ondaatje, Sebald, Bidart, Carson, Lynne Tillman, Geoffrey O'Brien, Luc Sante, Jenny Boully, Lisa Robertson, Ander Monson, among so many others—there's also a specifically essayistic impulse in a lot of the strongest recent fiction and poems. When you finish many of the books I most like, you often don't know exactly what they were: fiction, nonfiction, poetry, or an essay masquerading as a poem or as a novel, whatever.

AG: The voice in Hollywood & God is at times almost like an actor inhabiting various persona. "Into one life and out another," you write in the title poem. In your introduction to your Everyman's Library edition of James Cain, you quote Cain as saying, "But to write anything, I have to pretend to be somebody else." Was this a conscious strategy in writing Hollywood & God, or is it inherent to how you write?
RP: I think it is more inherent in how I work, and how I think and feel. This wasn't a conscious strategy adopted for a project. In the Jim Thompson book, for instance, I was fascinated by oral history. I realized early on I should put whatever information I found in the voices of the people I talked to, those who, in a sense, owned that information. What I discovered listening to and transcribing all the tapes was that my sources talked in ways that were so much more original and idiosyncratic than the same information would sound if a biographer flattened it out.

In *Hollywood & God* I was interested in telling other people's stories in what looks like my voice and my stories in what looks like other people's voices. I think the shifts of identity in *Hollywood & God*—the moments where suddenly the narrative voice of a poem gives way to another character—is one of the root elements of the book. Recurrently, I was aiming for a collective or composite voice, and there's inevitably a lot of collage. At one point in the title poem, I say, "this hour I tell you things in confidence / I might not tell everybody, but I'll tell you," but those lines are a quotation from Whitman, from a poem called, interestingly enough, "Song of Myself." So, the confession is actually his, though it looks like mine, and part of the pleasure in quoting those lines is that Whitman sounds there less like Whitman and more like Gertrude Stein, who's also quoted in the poem, from a book titled—again, interestingly enough—*Everybody's Autobiography*. Often, when it appears I'm talking, it's actually someone else, another writer, or a movie, song, interview or magazine article. I think that's inherent in how we all are, variously individual, fractured and composite.

AG: There's a lot of identity and even gender switching in *Hollywood & God*. I think this has something to do with your interest in performance—whether actors or musicians—and the idea that we all play different roles. But it also seems to go deeper than this to a sense of identity as fundamentally unsettled.

RP: That's absolutely true. There's something eternally in-process about them, the identities in this book, and I suppose "identity" in general. I think, perhaps because of a century of movies, popular music, and eventually television and the Internet—but Ovid obviously knew this also—there's a way that when you open your mouth you really don't know who's talking, for us—what movie, song, TV program, or memoir we're inadvertently ventriloquizing. At no moment in history has so much culture been available to people—books, recordings, films, the Internet—what isn't available?

. . . Well, where's the DVD of *City of Sadness*? But that's another question.

Our glut of culture and information is important for writing along at least two related strands. First, that glut very much connects to this notion of identity we're talking about, who we really are, what sort of world we really inhabit, and the resources we need as writers to represent ourselves inside and against that world. Second, I think that glut is probably also the oddest and most persistent tangent of literary modernism. The world the average person inhabits today, and not just mainly as a result of Internet, resembles a modernist work of literature. Our everyday world is full of collage and unreliable narrators; it's multiple-voiced, and there are all sorts of vernaculars and claims to authority or power to be negotiated. I think we haven't come to terms yet with the consequences of this. The situation we're in now is probably similar to one hundred years ago. The transformation that the individual, the self and society went through as result of their new cultural technologies—such as electricity, film, the telephone, the automobile, all the rest—is something that we are playing out on overdrive with our new twenty-first-century technologies.

AG: In the poem "Sister Elvis" from *Hollywood & God*, a female Elvis Presley impersonator—described in the first person—briefly becomes a priest-like figure. This

transformation from secular to sacred and back again seems central to the book and is signaled by its title.

RP: She's sort of the book in miniature, as I saw it, or at least a distillation of crucial aspects of the book. You have, on the one hand, her insane obsession with Elvis Presley to the point of totally remaking her life in imitation of him. And, on the other, you have her way of talking about Elvis that derives from American religion, particularly TV preachers, and sermons. I was interested in what happens if you pursue that connection and mix those two things together. Or if you put Cotton Mather next to T.D. Rice.

There's also the matter of my own implication in these issues. As I'm fond of saying, just about everything I know about literature, art, even life, I suppose, I learned from The Kinks back in high school and college. So, I wouldn't deny at all that I haven't thought, and don't even now think, of people like Ray Davies, Bob Dylan, Elvis Costello, Lee Wiley, Arthur Alexander, Maria Callas, or Ma Rainey from my own lifetime the way Sister Elvis thinks of Elvis Presley. That's true of writers and artists, also. Beckett, Warhol, Merrill, Barthelme, Borges—I was nothing in high school and college if not a fan. Some of what I'm saying goes back to the book's interest in the relationship between the living and the dead. I have sentimentality about my dear dead, starting with family and friends, and moving outward into writers and artists who are a crucial part of my inner life. As I said, it's sort of how I view poetry and writing, as a conversation between the living and the dead. *Hollywood & God* is a book of ghosts, starting off with a poem spoken by someone who you discover in the last line of the poem is probably dead. The elegy in there for my father-in-law, "Pacific Coast Highway," is a poem about what might happen to the spirit in the moment of sudden death. The September 11 poem, "Last Seen," is a more public reckoning of that same moment.

AG: Your father is a recurring, complicated figure in *Hollywood & God*. Without necessarily speaking autobiographically, can you say what a father figure might represent for you, as well as for your reader?

RP: My father was a remarkable person in so many ways. He was among the smartest and most decent people I ever met. He worked for the post office in Boston, a supervisor in the old South Station PO, and I loved visiting him there in his office on the mezzanine with the trains, crowds, newsstands, Red Caps and shoe shine boys bustling below him. In the last years of his life, because he was so good at what he did, he became a troubleshooter sent around from post office to post office. But there was something immensely thwarted and furtive about him that I still don't fully understand to this day. During high school, when I would talk to him about the books that had been assigned, I noticed that he had read every single one up until a certain moment in time, roughly 1950, and then literally nothing at all after that. After he got out of the service, my aunt once told me that he read five or six books from the library a week. But suddenly that stopped. When my own interests—probably as a consequence of my father's still-burbling enthusiasm for books—started to move more seriously in that direction, my relationship with him got troubled, competitive and full of anger, with mutual suspicions, charges and recriminations. That coincided with a lot of similar things going on in the world, as this was the late 1960s and early '70s. We never got back on track. He died when I was in grad school. Our relationship was frozen there until not so long ago, when I realized that if he had lived, that kind of inner-embalming sense of where things were with us couldn't have persisted and that, oddly, I was more or less where he would have wanted if either of us had been calm enough to see what was in front of us. If he had lived longer, at some point we would have had to deal with each other in different ways.

There are multiple father figures in the book, with various, sometimes conflicting histories and biographies. In the Barbara Peyton piece, the father works in Los Angeles, also for the post office, but his moonlighting job is as a bartender at The Coach and Horses on Sunset, whereas my own father's was at Siegel's Shoes, a woman's shoe store with branches in downtown Boston and Quincy Square. I don't know whether my father ever was in Los Angeles, certainly not during my childhood with me, but that piece is a re-imagining of who he was, and a kind of fantasy accounting for my own interests in people like Barbara Peyton, and the B-movies she was in. Elsewhere there's more of my physical experience of growing up in Boston. The final piece, "Shame," is about trying to flip over everything else in the book about my father and come at what it might have been like to be him, why he was the way he was. What I hope comes across is a tremendous honoring of the yearning for family that was in my father, and that I didn't really see until recently.

AG: You've edited two volumes of noir fiction, as well as written a biography of Jim Thompson. You're obviously interested in tough guys, but I'm also struck by your attention to the frailty of their masculinity and masculinity as a kind of fiction. Can you talk about this?
RP: One of the surprises of my research for *Savage Art* was that someone like Jim Thompson possessed an almost dysfunctional sensitivity and vulnerability. I was amazed to learn from his two sisters how reluctant he was to do his own true crime

research, because the painful stories upset him so much—his drinking likely comes out of that sensitivity, as do his own violent novels. I think that masculinity in America is not only a fiction, as you say, but a largely pernicious, damaging fiction. I think my father felt he must live up to the role of the conventional American family man, and that was tremendously destructive for him, because his own impulses and inclinations moved in more complicated directions. Also, in *Hollywood & God*, a lot of times when you first think a man must be talking, you then realize it's a woman. It's one of the trap doors of identity and personality that the reader falls through into another psychic, sexual space.

AG: In *Hollywood & God*, movies are reality, and reality is like a movie. Yet I don't think this is so much an illustration of Guy Debord's notion of the "society of the spectacle" but of the way we structure our reality around narratives and consciously or unconsciously inhabit certain roles.
RP: More than fifty years later, *The Society of the Spectacle* still seems the most convincing media theory and most incisive description of the world we actually now inhabit. It's extremely hard to be naïve about one's own and even apparently most impulsive gestures after reading *The Society of the Spectacle*. Maybe what my book tentatively explores is what it's like for at least some of us—living or fictional, if that distinction makes a difference here—to speak from inside the society of the spectacle. The psychic consequences of inhabiting a world that is so charged, so volatile, so slippery, so disenchanted. But, as I said, I live in that world, too. It's not satire. I'm not on the outside taking shots at the poor deluded people inside. I'm one of them. I think we're all one of them. I don't know how you could not be one of them at this point. Debord himself ended up a myth—his recent cultural currency is very "society of the spectacle," isn't it? He's next year's Che Guevara.

AG: In this sense, *Hollywood & God* isn't so much a critique of either Hollywood or religion, but instead seems to hold the best aspects of each in relatively high esteem, while at the same time recognizing and describing their dark underbellies.
RP: I think spiritual impulses are essentially honorable, however disastrous or contradictory often is their expression. I was interested in tracking and exploring these impulses across our turn-of-the-century American life, against the backdrop and residues and ruins of my own Catholic childhood, and that meant embodying it, or at least trying to embody it, from as many angles as possible.

I think one of the darkest passages in the book is also one of the most spiritually transcendent moments of the book, and that's the ending of "Sister Elvis." She ultimately produces this shroud on a napkin after not only cutting herself but convincing herself as well that she's seeing Elvis's face in the rain and dirt of a motel window. That moment, like so many other instances in the book, could easily be turned into a joke, but I didn't view it as a joke. Or just a joke. She's also like one of the great martyrs, Saint Catherine of Sienna, and all the others that the nuns and Jesuits avidly paraded before us in school. Spiritual impulses are anything but trivial, but neither of course is Hollywood.

AG: The editors of *The Literary Review* specifically wanted me to interview you for this issue and its theme of "Manifest Destiny." What form, if any, does "Manifest Destiny" take in the United States in the year 2009?

RP: Let me try to think about this by trying to talk about Barack Obama. The only figure I've ever seen remotely like him is Bob Dylan. Both are totally self-invented people who early on against all possible odds and against any historical, geographical, cultural or even genetic predictions for them possessed an astonishingly large and precise sense of their own destiny. When you read his autobiography, you see that Obama is almost uncannily self-invented. There was nothing inherent about Barry Obama becoming Barack Obama—and it's not all that easy to locate Barry inside Barack. I'd love to have met him as he was leaving Occidental College to come to New York and Columbia, which is when and where this self-invention seems to have focused. Similarly, I think about Robert Zimmerman coming out of Hibbing, Minnesota, and making himself into Bob Dylan. Both men created a possibility of who they could be and what they might do through their imaginations and wills, and then became that possibility. Obama is also the first president who lives in the same language world that you and I do as writers. He has a sense of craft, but also of historical and rhetorical context, of quick, mercurial allusions, even, as we were saying before, of identity as a sort of collage, and that's part of what makes him seem so modern and classic at once. There's something about him that is always thinking of himself and locating himself in other people and the words of other creators—not only on the page, but even more in his speeches. In a single sentence of that speech he gave in Grant Park on election night, he was able to summon King, Kennedy, Roosevelt and Lincoln without exactly quoting any of them. I have never witnessed anything like it—unless it's Dylan similarly summoning America's musical past inside the textures of his songs.

Maybe Obama and Dylan represent the flip side of Manifest Destiny, at least historical American Manifest Destiny. Dylan even puns on this in his autobiography, *Chronicles*: "My destiny was manifest," is how I remember he put it. During the past eight years, it was almost too easy to view America as a sociopathic parody of Manifest Destiny, a crazed empire on a brutal spree. But Obama is trying to imagine another America, and if what he's trying to do works, the country that emerges will look entirely different from now. His is a much humbler, much more empathetic notion of what a country and a people are.

Yet what Obama accomplished in his own life, with his reinvention of the possibilities of his life, isn't all that different in design than the Manifest Destiny of a continent, or a nation reinventing itself. Manifest Destiny, as I understand it, involves those same kinds of acts of the imagination and will: these are the possibilities for this space, this nation, and how we will inhabit it.

You dig deep enough and all you get is mysteries, wonders and surprises that turn out to be inevitable and destined.

Paul Yoon
Once the Shore

Reviewed by Marion Wyce

In Paul Yoon's debut collection of linked short stories, *Once the Shore*, we explore the fictional island of Solla, off the coast of South Korea, traversing not only its varied topography but also its complex history. We begin at a coastal resort in the present, then find ourselves at sea in 1947, then again in the present, further inland, near the forest. Solla is constant, with Tamra Mountain at its center, ancient caves, and, of course, the vast sea that surrounds and defines it. Yet Solla is ever changing, its inhabitants adapting to the occupying forces of first the Japanese and American militaries, and later, wealthy foreign tourists. As the collection shifts in time and space, we have the sense that time is not strictly linear here—that the past is never quite past, that everything is part of what has happened here before and what has yet to happen.

So it is with the first two stories, separated in time by fifty years but with a strikingly similar tragic event at their centers: the sudden, violent death of a loved one in an accident caused by the American military. In the title story, selected for *The Best American Short Stories 2006*, a young waiter, Jim, cannot accept that his brother has been killed at sea because his body hasn't been recovered: "Until then, his brother was still fishing." Jim's loss takes on greater poignancy as we slip backward in time to 1947 and encounter the family of another missing fisherman in "Among the Wreckage." Karo is one of a hundred men missing—and presumably killed—by errant US bomb testing just east of Solla. Each story in Yoon's collection builds on the ones that sur-

Sarabande Books: Louisville, KY, 2009.

round it, so that we are left to consider not just the deaths of these two men, but what it means to live in a place where fishermen become collateral damage. But loss is always awful in its specificity, and as much as Jim's brother and Karo become part of the larger story of Solla, the people who grieve them want to reclaim them from the anonymity of death. As the accident becomes the stuff of chatter among Jim's coworkers at the resort, he keeps his loss to himself to "regain his brother, pull him back down from the static of the sea and air. From the mouths of strangers." Karo's elderly parents are on a more tangible recovery mission, setting off in a fishing boat together to find their son, hoping he has somehow survived. The brilliance of Yoon's writing is his ability to collapse an entire relationship into a singular, haunting image. The couple's marriage has been marked by silences, and distance has grown between them. Yet, husband and wife are as one in the story's final, brutal lines, working together as a seamless "they," their individuality disappearing: "When a body passed them, they reached for the man. Some they held by the feet, others by the arms, neck, or hair. Whatever was closest. They picked them as if for harvest... And, with all their effort, they pulled the floating men closer and lifted their still faces out of the water."

Thus loss divides and connects. Everyone in Solla seems to be haunted by loss: death at war, death by fire, death by heart attack, an arm lost to a tiger shark, a lame leg. Throughout the collection we encounter unlikely pairings of damaged people who find comfort together as they confront the ghosts of their pasts. In "So That They Do Not Hear Us," an aging sea woman, Ahrim, who earns her living diving, has befriended a boy who lost his left arm to a tiger shark. He seems to let other children taunt him, and Ahrim thinks she knows why: "Because he was afraid. Because his life was governed by an incident that occurred at sea, as though his days were a preparation for when it would happen again, embodied in a multitude of shapes and forms and places." She could nearly be describing herself, however, haunted as she remains by the war death of her husband forty-five years earlier. At the story's end, she shares a moment with the boy as he practices diving in the safety of her bathtub: "He lay motionless, the water clear. She inhaled and, in her imagination, joined him."

Yet other people are always a mystery, couplings never complete, our desire to connect straining against the limits of our imagination. Yoon is interested in the way that even the most familiar is ultimately unknowable and strange. We are told that Solla is an island where "the distance from one destination to another never took longer than an hour by car." But even in such a circumscribed place, there is unexplored terrain, rumors of secret passageways hidden among the island's caves. An American tourist who befriends the waiter Jim in "Once the Shore" asks him to take her to see one of these caves, which figures in a story that has formed part of the lore of her marriage. Her husband has recently died, and she is left with the feeling that she never really knew him, at least not after he came home from the war. She tells Jim, "the man whom I knew, he never came. So I want to remember him. Not the one who returned. But the one who never left." A story is what she's after, a narrative of her own life that makes sense to her. So it's only fitting that, in the final scene, Jim hands her a stone and watches as she uses it to write on the wall of the cave, perhaps "the words of a language long forgotten."

But on Yoon's island of Solla, it seems that nothing is ever really gone. As we move forward and backward in time, absence and presence become inseparable parts of a rhythm, as natural as the coming and going of the tides. In the final story, "The Hanging Lanterns of Ido," a man named Taeho is told by a waitress that he looks just like another man she knew who has died. "She thought you were a ghost," his wife tells him, saying it must have been "an awful thing." At the story's end, however, Taeho insists to his wife, "If you ever go away, I will remember your face . . . And I will look for it." Maybe a haunting, these stories suggest, is nothing to be feared. Maybe our ghosts are just a sign that nothing we lose ever truly leaves us.

Pasha Malla
The Withdrawal Method

Reviewed by Jeff Bursey

The thirteen stories that make up Pasha Malla's first book of fiction take place in unremarkable households, hospitals, streets, a dry Niagara Falls, and assorted other places that have an atmosphere familiar to Canadians. Yet, there is nothing border-patrolled about the concerns in these stories: boredom, loss, regret and death are universal. *The Withdrawal Method* is, from its surface to its core, a work that concentrates on details instead of presenting a large picture, and this may strike some as unambitious. It is, rather, an intense and satisfying concentration on what we might consider humdrum or mundane matters.

In its series of small canvases there is an ever-present need on the part of minor and major characters to connect with others, or to understand why there is no connection anymore. Displays of deep affection are intermittent, sadness prevails, and intimacy is infrequent. Sex, when it occurs, is often masturbatory instead of with a partner. Most prevalent are neighborliness and scenes of communal meals where blood relations and adopted parties alike are important.

"The Past Composed" has Les living with his sister, Judy, after incidents have ended the life he knew, and their small unit briefly and suddenly expands to include a boy named Pico who likes to hang around. Board games, often a marker of family unity, recur, in this case not Clue or Monopoly but, appropriately, Trouble. Yet connections get severed, or are endangered, and the general mood is of a Sunday after-

Soft Skull Press: New York, NY, 2009.

noon when you have a slight headache, just before spring begins, with the land starting to smell earthy but mucky snow persisting in shadow-covered grass.

Malla employs the technique of providing specific descriptions to show how certain characters are tuned in to the close workings of the world (perhaps a reflection of his own concentration on writing). "Timber watched the crosswalk sign change from man to flashing hand," goes one paragraph in "Timber on the Wheel of Everyone," linking him to the obsessive nine-year-old narrator, Big Gal, of "Pushing Oceans In and Pulling Oceans Out" who regularly says things like: "I make sure the games are all square on the shelf. The edges have to be even and matched up equally, which is called symmetry. We learned it in math." This attention to the *whatness* of the everyday ripens in "Dizzy When You Look Down," a story about basketball games played by someone with sketchily-described revolutionary motivations.

What Malla does right in certain stories is allow himself the freedom to not sound like many Canadian writers aged thirty to forty-five who have been force-fed the gruel of Raymond Carver, Alice Munro et al., instead of richer and more substantial authors like William Gaddis and Gilbert Sorrentino. Here and there Malla introduces the fantastic and the offbeat, or allows himself to display a sense of humor that leavens the grimness of the material.

"The Slough," the collection's first story, keeps the reader nicely off balance, and amused, in the third-person beginning where a woman tells her boyfriend that she's going to lose her skin due a topical cream. "Topical? Do you mean like up-to-date? Current?" This kind of set-up and wordplay is promising. "Big City Girls" shows Alex, a young boy, having his head messed with by his sister's friends' sex game and the potential ramifications. As seen by Alex very near the end, the girls outside look "as though someone had cut their pictures from a magazine and laid them down there, one by one, side by side." That is a subtle and incisive comment, or prognostication, almost an aside, a technique employed well in other places.

Many stories center on an impulse to unite. For variety, Malla shows in "Long Short Short Long" one boy's cruelty to another (who persists in calling him a friend), and how that same tormentor later imagines a connection with a teacher that is unhealthy. Here, as elsewhere, Malla's reliance on details about an average-day-in-an-average-life—a restrained ambit—marks him out as a domestic novelist, and that is meant as a compliment. He keeps his eye on siblings, fathers, and men and women whose lives take bad turns or peter out. Politics, the economy, war and world events don't intrude save for an eco-disaster that, one suspects, led to the drying up of Niagara Falls. Malla has a big tent approach and is not, on the evidence of *The*

Withdrawal Method, interested in devising gigantic self-explanatory systems like those found in the fictions of Thomas Pynchon, Joseph McElroy, or Don DeLillo. Family is the first, and at times uncomfortable, refuge from systems, cruelty, and sadness; while it contains its potential for hurt and disappointment, it can also serve to keep one going when the world is too difficult.

The domestic aspect shows itself, among other ways, in how Malla layers the emotionality of men. To choose an illustrative example from one story, the widowed father in "Pushing Oceans In and Pulling Oceans Out" has to clean up his mentally challenged seven-year-old son. "My dad Greg gets home at 5:58 and smells Brian right away and goes, Woo-wee buddy! He picks Brian up over one shoulder like a fireman and carries him upstairs. The tub goes on. I can hear them both laughing from my spot at the kitchen table and the water splashing around while my dad Greg washes the crap off my brother." Often, fiction presents this as woman's work, and as a depressing scene; instead, we're shown tenderness and the love of father for his son.

In "The Film We Made About Dads" (its title reminiscent of Curtis White's *Memories of My Father Watching TV*) there is this passage: "When it was time for the children to move away from home, the dads were strong. The wives wept in the driveways as the children pulled away in cars with couches strapped to the roofs, and the dads held the wives and stroked their hair. It would later be easy for us to erase the tears that ran down the dads' faces. We have computer programs for that sort of business." What we may be reading in this passage is a quiet rebuke to writers who programmatically erase emotional nuances from men, leaving them as caricatures expressing only anger, despair or coldness.

Malla's engagement with the softer emotions felt by men, especially, is a strength of the fiction. Aligned to this is the overall calmness of the collection's tone, even where a character feels extreme emotions. There is a catholic aspect to Malla's view of the world. The use of playful humor helps, as the men don't come out looking anything other than human; it functions on both the technical and human levels, and is sometimes missing in contemporary fiction. Humor's sharper bite is present in "Respite" where the life of a novelist is portrayed. "But Womack was writing a novel, and he was doing good work. He had written more than one hundred pages. The words were coming. Sentences spilled into paragraphs spilled into chapters, while on the periphery Adriane came in and out of the apartment like the mechanical bird in a windup clock."

Nicolas Pesquès
Juliology

Reviewed by Paul-Victor Winters

Poet and translator Cole Swensen's crisp rendering of Nicolas Pesquès's *Juliology*, originally published in French as part of a larger volume, exposes a sparse, decided grammar that is both emotional and intellectual. The collection, which may be seen as a sort of *ars poetica*, continues Pesquès's examination of one mountain, Juliau, in the Ardèche region of south-central France. These poems, however, resonate without consideration of that premise.

The topic at hand is language itself—its relationship to speaker, place, and meaning. The slender volume presents one long single poem in sections. The common speaker of the pieces may be the poet himself, considering "how to repair what language has sundered." He offers sometimes odd, but insightful commentary on writing and on reading:

> writing is based only on what gives way

> writing through weakness, into the yellow, to open the heart
> one hand in artifice the other in the dark
> and perfect pitch turned to grammar

Pesquès suggests that fact and fiction converge, and that we are

> always trying to come up with a single version
> a version made impossible by language
> by the autonomy of grammar.

Counterpath Press: Denver, CO, 2008.

This, it seems, is the impact of language on our lives; consider "the eye, the sentence, tarnished by the breath of perception." Language is simply inadequate—or, at best, as the Deconstructionists would have it, lacking any fixed, certain meaning. What other tools exist, however, in our quest to clarify the meaning evident in the world that surrounds us?

In Swensen's deft rendering, language is occasionally able to sharply render meaning. Its insufficiencies give way to motifs and slowly-evolving concepts. Here is where landscape enters—"there where forest and sentence will co-exist," where "the view has turned to words." One sees the geography of concept mapped out, and the thought process seems one of routing and rerouting. This speaker struggles throughout:

> I insist that writing lead not only to a moving end
> but that it also mark an ascension, a nervous terminus that mumbles
> in the field with branching fangs.

And then:

> Something inconsolable. A cognitive pain. A poem like that.
> That tracks down reason wherever it's insoluble, wherever it can't be
> ratified: beyond sensation . . .

The fact that these poems are translated from the French is not the only reason a reader may be reminded of the French Symbolists. Despite the hollowness of language, it brings us, hopefully, to understanding. Unlike the Symbolists, however, there is no dichotomy between poet (or speaker) and subject, and no dichotomy between the inner and outer self. Eventually, we see this speaker's conflict with reason and sense-making fully at odds with language:

> Hypnotic eyes.
> Unstapling weather; grafting beyond-language.
>
> It such as.
>
> Disappeared, cross.
>
> The Deconstructionists may have been right.

Mallarmè said "to name is to destroy." Pesquès's speaker, ultimately, seems just to be trying to make sense of things. It is, ultimately, a challenge for one to make sense of the world using language: "Sensation goes metallic. Advances through the hardened language. / Making sure the body doesn't get off lightly." Pesquès, his speaker, and his readers are left, then, with "one word in the sentence, one in the throat."

Dunya Mikhail
Diary of A Wave Outside the Sea

Reviewed by Deborah Hall

Reading Dunya Mikhail's lyrical and poetic memoir *Diary of A Wave Outside the Sea* is like diving into a watery, dreamy world. One must leave behind rationale, urges for temporal grounding and a reliance on facts. Mikhail pulls you into her impressionistic world like a strong tide, tossing the reader about with strong visuals, sensitive perspectives, poetic questions, snippets, and philosophic observations:

> Every sorrow and mistake adds up
> to a tally of daily ruination.
> And nothing is as long as memories' shadow

Not only does Mikhail's narrative content resist precise meaning, but her text resists a formal taxonomy. Even if demarcations and definitions of memoir were as fluid as her verse, any critic would struggle to classify this Arab-American, Iraqi-born writer. It's true that the work is memoir, and if I could leave it at that, I would. For the most part, Mikhail resists narrative conventions of scene and anecdote: fictional techniques that memoirists usually employ. She uses verse to narrate the fragments into a blended whole.

In fact, the structure of this memoir seems influenced by the ancient Mesopotamian literary form of *maqáma*. The *maqámát* (plural) were a series of rhymed verses told orally in order to pass along knowledge. Seekers of knowledge

Translated from Arabic by Elizabeth Winslow, and Dunya Mikhail. New Directions: New York, NY, 2009.

had to journey in order to hear and learn from speakers. Its name (meaning "he stood") relates to the act of oration, standing to perform the verse. Mikhail might be reminding the reader of her birthplace's deep connection to forms of early literature.

The poetic form she employs is also similar to the Homeric epic poem. Actually, the tablets of the epic poem of Gilgamesh, which predate Homer, were found in a temple in the city of Nineveh—now contemporary Mosul, Iraq. The tablets are written in the ancient language of Akkadian (a cuneiform language) which was replaced by Aramaic, a language Mikhail's family still speaks. It is not peculiar then that a large part of Part One deals with the mythic story of Gilgamesh.

Memoirs about migration or integration often have similar themes: a difficult journey; a path of self-discovery; individual heroism; and issues of identity, marginality and alienation as well as nostalgia for the native land. For the Arab-American female, there is also an expectation by Western readers to address the status of women in Muslim society as well as right-wing eccentricities of the Islamic faith. But Mikhail is a Christian Iraqi and sets out with no such intentions of situating herself in a genre. She is certainly an immigrant, but she doesn't address issues of marginality and identity, nor does she defend or explain Arab stereotypes to a Western reader. Alienation is present, but it's due to the circumstances of war and censorship in the native homeland rather than the adopted land. In Mikhail's experience, war and censorship bring the creatively-inclined together in Iraq (at the *souq*, the Writer's Union, or the cinema club). Rather than feelings of separation, this memoir paints moments of connectivity within her circle of friends espousing a humanity and community that hints of a global connectivity more evocative of the poetry of Rumi than such classic Arab-American autobiographies as Edward Said's *Out of Place: A Memoir* or Leila Ahmed's *A Border Passage: From Cairo to America—A Woman's Journey* which address the dominate themes mentioned above. This is not to say that Mikhail's work trumps these texts. I don't mean to compare and rank. Said and Ahmed's autobiographical works are crucial texts for postcolonial and women's studies because they cross literary lines into politics, history, sociology, religion and culture, to name a few. But Mikhail is a poet who renders her world poetically and philosophically, without overt arguments, by curious wondering and questioning, disarming the reader with an impact that feels more like an impression than a factual knowing.

Like immigrant memoirs, nostalgia for a lost homeland is expressed although Mikhail determines to leave Iraq without looking back. Her longing, however, is for a pre-war period in Iraq that doesn't exist anymore. She certainly doesn't idealize the war-weary Baghdad that continues today in turmoil. From her teens until she leaves as an adult, she has experienced the Iran-Iraq War (1980-1988), the invasion of Kuwait in 1990, and the First Gulf War in 1991.

Diary of a Wave is fragmented, and drifts along seemingly without temporal anchor although its divisions (two parts) point toward periods of time. It's a feminist memoir in that it expresses a female creative mind experiencing a male world. But unlike many feminist texts, it doesn't wrestle with domination, subordination or resistance like the more infamous Nawal El Saadawi of Egypt whose novel *Woman At Point Zero* memorializes in story one woman's resistance, courage and revenge against a patriarchal system just before she is sentenced to death. But Mikhail's philosophic questions can be even more politically affective:

> What kind of hands sprinkle death over the trees
> So that grains of wheat fall from shivering beaks
> And the bulging eyes of birds
> Stiffen with broken eggs?

Like Georgia O'Keefe's paintings, Mikhail subsumes her body with the landscape: "The streets crawl, intersecting in the veins of my hands." Like O'Keefe's microscopic vision of flowers, Mikhail influences the reader's perspective: "I felt pity for the realist ... so I reversed the lens / and made the trees look nearer / until they appeared their natural size / and were threatened once again by the chattering of the birds." You feel lopsided in Mikhail's world. She is destabilizing to a reality-based, war-is-a-necessary-evil world.

The first part of this two-part verse memoir is dated 1991–1994 in Iraq. Just when you think her world is pure poetic myth where Zeus, Gilgamesh and Prometheus make appearances, she reminds you that the world is a place where "planes flew over shelters / Over the children who slept under the debris / Over the body parts that had been children" and you are not swimming so languidly anymore. She asks:

> I wonder how Santa Claus of the twentieth century felt
> when he carried a sack of shells to the children of Iraq?
> And how did he feel when they gave him back the sack
> filled with such presents
> > as a mutilated finger
> a red braid
> a torn book
> a damaged toy
> a card of protest?

The list builds until the reader's breath has slowed—each image a symbol of childhood destroyed or disrupted. And when she states, "In war, no one is rescued from death. / The killed die physically / and the killers die morally," she is indicting the act of war—criticizing the heroism and medals that men bestow upon each other. She makes it personal when she asks, "O Pilot, you have the power / to demolish a human being in the dark / but do you have the ability to defeat the night / that descends on the heart?" She knows the answer, and the reader knows, too. It is a feminine, multilayered response that crosses physical zones subverting enemy-killing to the simplest angle, a child's:

The child rose and asked his mother:
—What are enemies, Mama?
—They are those ghosts
who stand behind the line,
pointing their guns at the moon.

When the child realizes that by shooting the moon and sometimes hitting half, leaving a crescent, or sometimes making the moon disappear altogether, that the enemies are destroying the same moon that is also theirs, the mother explains:

And this is called sacrifice.
They sacrifice what they have
in order to annihilate what we have.

It is hard to capture the full effect of immersion into Mikhail's world. It is one in which the idea of Saddam's henchmen blur together with American pilots who drop bombs. Interestingly, Part One of this memoir was first published in Iraq in 1995 by the Ministry of Culture (the former title was *Journal of a Wave Outside the Sea*). As government officials realized the content was not supportive of Saddam, Mikhail's visa came through.

Before Part One ends, Mikhail has developed a metaphor for protecting the psyche of children and artists/poets who wish to preserve their sanity: that of living in a shell, rejecting a male-centered reality. I have to admit that interpreting Mikhail's meaning feels a little false. She is more mercurial than any memoirist I've read; her writing resists being pinned down, and yet I am working here to pin her down. If I say, for instance, by the end of Part One that she is trapped in a shell, I mean she is in a glass box, and I also mean she is still in the dream holding onto hope: "I have spent a long time here, / holding a candle that never goes out, never / melts." Each is true and false. I can't tell whether I've been slapped or sung to sleep with a lullaby. That's Mikhail's effect.

If Part One is poetically destabilizing, mesmerizing, and impressionistic, Part Two (1995–2007) is more reality-based: it grounds with people, places and events.

Mikhail begins with a narrative of departure, waiting for a visa. When she gets out of Iraq (at age thirty one), she carries her world in a suitcase; that is, she carries letters, poems and photographs. The next series of flashbacks inspired by the items in her bag is not unlike Tim O'Brien's *The Things They Carried*, in which stories are told via the tangible and intangible things soldiers carry in war. In this way, Part Two, which is about coming to America, focuses on what and who she leaves behind. Here we learn anecdotes that enable us to imagine living in Baghdad, working as a journalist as well as the frustrations of a dictatorial system in which you are always waiting for permission from a government official. In Mikhail's case, she waits to transfer her dying father to a hospital that can treat his kidney failure. The paperwork never goes through despite much effort.

Like many immigrant writers, Mikhail suffers from the guilt of escaping a war-torn home and feels the dichotomous split between new land and homeland. Yet, she writes like one unafraid, as if she never lived in an oppressive regime. When she relates skipping class to meet her young love when he was home on leave from the army, she describes the class as "the boring class on national culture that enforced the ideology of the Baath party." However, this memoir is no harangue against the politically obvious. It is true that its pages are filled with startling imagery and those images remind the reader of our common humanity and the insanity of war, but this memoir is a bridge connecting dreamers everywhere; it is a bridge from America to Iraq by way of introducing to the American reader so many poets we might not otherwise know.

We meet Hassan, a philosophic soldier who thinks computers will save Iraqis. When he is killed, we feel his loss. We meet Mikhail's friends from the university, her boyfriend, Mazin, and her friends from the garden of the Writers Union. We learn of the poet Ali Abdul Amiir and his love of Fairouz, the great Lebanese singer, of the poet Munthir Abdul-Hur, who called Mikhail "sister" and who was always searching for Jan Dammo, the absent-minded poet who never held a job and always fell asleep at the wrong times when he served in the army. We meet female Iraqi poets, getting quick introductions that leave us wanting more. As these names pile up, we feel the loss of friendships, the nostalgia for home and the loneliness that immigrants bear.

At the memoir's end, we find Mikhail in America finally having a life after many years of delay (she is reunited with Mazin after ten years apart). She is a mother and has much to say about America. She sees its dichotomy: its youthful aggression, and how it means well. She writes, "America bombs with one hand / and shelters with the other." We see ourselves better through her clear eyes.

The last stanza celebrates the mixing of two cultures and tips a hat to the passage of childhood, a holy time in Mikhail's world, through her daughter's filter:

> Larsa catters the old pictures
> and mixes them with the new ones.
> She mixes pictures of snowballs in Michigan
> with pictures of a round city with two rivers
> palm trees
> poetry
> wars
> a thousand and one nights.
> Inside that city was our home,
> inside the home was our garden
> not separated from the neighbors even by a wall,
> and inside that garden was a razqui flower
> I will never smell again.

This Iraqi-American poet creates an experience for the reader that imitates the creative mind, re-visions cultural myths and reverses the dominant male-oriented perspective of reality, begging humanity to wake up to her dream. In Mikhail's dream we would all share the beneficial light of the moon, celebrating our common humanity, and there would certainly be no war.

Ernesto Cardenal and Jonathan Cohen, editors
Pluriverse: New and Selected Poems

Reviewed by Kristina Marie Darling

Pluriverse: New and Selected Poems offers readers an introduction to the literary career of Nicaraguan activist, priest, and ambassador Ernesto Cardenal. Spanning fifty-four years of the author's work, this comprehensive volume includes selections of his documentary poems, romantic epigraphs, and religious writings. Although formally diverse, these works are gracefully unified through an exploration of the possible intersection between political and spiritual life. Presenting a vision of social change rooted in a higher sense of purpose, Cardenal's poems address Nicaragua's turbulent history while adeptly situating this history within a broader literary and philosophical context.

In his documentary historical poems, for example, Cardenal continually returns to personal religious experiences as a source of insight about larger political structures, suggesting an affinity between one's inner life and the manner in which social change is enacted. Subtly complicating the pragmatic ways many of his contemporaries conceived of reform, Cardenal's work presents a self-reflexive alternative, which he describes with lyricism and precision throughout. In "Give Ear to My Words (Psalm 5)," the poet depicts disingenuousness as being the weakness of the current regime, suggesting that intent often governs outcome in political life. He writes,

> At the hour of the Alarm Siren
> you will be with me
> you will be my refuge on the day of the Bomb

Translated from Spanish by Mireya Jaimes-Freyre, John Lyons, Thomas Merton, Robert Pring-Mill, Kenneth Rexroth, and Donald D. Walsh. New Directions: New York, NY, 2009.

> You bless the righteous
> who don't believe in the lies of their ads
> nor in their publicity and political campaigns
> Your love surrounds them
> > like armored tanks

Here, Cardenal conflates the speaker's interior existence with the events of the external world, suggesting an affinity between the two. By pairing psychological resistance to unjust authority, such as disbelief in "the lies of their ads," with imagery of "armored tanks" surrounding the speaker's adversary, Cardenal suggests that the former often gives way to the latter. Wonderfully meditative and consistently thought-provoking, the works within this collection balance introspection with political consciousness, forging unexpected connections between worldly and spiritual life.

Moreover, while conveying abstract ideas about the society he inhabits, Cardenal grounds his observations in concrete images, which often become loci for less tangible concepts. Throughout *Pluriverse*, commonplace items serve as a point of entry to significant questions about emergent social issues, allowing Cardenal to assess cultural trends with subtlety and wit.

In "A Prayer for Marilyn Monroe," the author depicts technology, media culture, and psychoanalysis as having replaced, for many young people, the notion of a higher purpose that he advocates throughout the book. Appealing to the definitive symbol of this new "religion" of glamour and self-interest, Cardenal calls for a more spiritually centered worldview, allowing tangible images to make these ambitious claims. He writes, for example,

> The film ended without the final kiss.
> She was found dead in her bed with her hand on the phone.
> And the detectives never learned who she was going to call.
> She was
> like someone who had dialed the number of the only friendly voice
> and only heard the voice of a recording that says: *WRONG NUMBER.*
> Or like someone who had been wounded by gangsters
> reaching for a disconnected phone.

Here, Cardenal suggests the sense of spiritual emptiness inherent in such a lifestyle, an idea that he conveys through the complex image of the starlet dying with a telephone in hand. As the poem unfolds, this everyday object comes to represent Monroe's ongoing dialogue with the values of her generation, which the speaker depicts as a perpetual illusion of a "friendly voice" on the other end of the line. "A Prayer for Marilyn Monroe," like other poems in this comprehensive volume, elegantly evokes the ethereal through the concrete, offering readers a graceful synthesis of the philosophical and the familiar.

Contributors

Uruguayan poet **Delmira Agustini** (Poem 112) is considered one of the greatest female Latin American poets of the early twentieth-century. Her books include *El libro blanco, Cantos de la mañana, El rosario de Eros* and *Los astros del abismo* (all published between 1907 and 1924). *Selected Poetry of Delmira Agustini: Poetics of Eros*, edited and translated by Alejandro Cáceres, offers a good representation of her work for English-language readers. She died in 1914.

R.A. Allen ("The Emerald Coast" 33) lives in Memphis. His fiction has appeared in *The Barcelona Review #64, Calliope, PANK, SinisterCity, Sniplits* (audio) and others; poetry in *Word Riot, The New York Quarterly, Pirene's Fountain* and others.

In addition to *The Most Beautiful Book in the World: 8 Novellas,* **Alison Anderson** (*translator,* "The Most Beautiful Book in the World" 97) has translated from French Sélim Nassib's novels, *I Loved You for Your Voice* and *The Palestinian Lover;* Amélie Nothomb's *Tokyo Fiancée,* and Muriel Barbery's bestselling novel *The Elegance of the Hedgehog.*

J.R. Angelella's ("In Memoriam" 127) received an MFA in Writing from the Bennington Writing Seminars at Bennington College. He is a regular contributor to *The Chapbook Review* and his short fiction has been published in *Twelve Stories, Hunger Mountain* and is forthcoming in *Fifth Wednesday Journal.* He lives in Brooklyn with his wife, Kate, and is at work on his first novel.

Renée Ashley (Books 188) is the author of four volumes of poetry; the latest, *Basic Heart,* was awarded the 2009 X.J. Kennedy Poetry Prize. She is poetry editor for *The Literary Review.*

Nina Berberova, (Poem 130) who died in 1993 at age ninety-two, is best known for her prose fiction and nonfiction, but she was also a poet, playwright and translator. She left Russia in 1922 and lived in Paris until 1950, when she came to the United States. English translations of her poetry have appeared in *Cyphers, Modern Poetry in Translation,* and *Salt.*

Alberto Blanco, (Poems 118) one of Mexico's most important poets, is the author of, among other books, *El corazón del instante*, a compilation of twelve volumes of poetry and *La hora y la neblina*, a second compilation of another twelve books of poetry. *Dawn of the Senses* is the most representative sample of his work available in English.

Jeff Bursey's (Books 209) articles, fiction and reviews have appeared in many Canadian, British and United States publications. His plays have been performed in Canada.

Kelly Cherry ("Her Life to Come" 7) is the author of seventeen books, eight chapbooks and two translations of classical plays. *Hazard and Prospect: New and Selected Poems*, was published by LSU Press in 2007.

Along with José Martí, Nicaraguan poet **Rubén Darío** (Poems 110) was a leader of the *Modernismo* literary movement that renovated Latin American poetry between 1885 and 1915. Darío's most important books are *Azul . . .* , *Cantos de vida y esperanza*, *El cisne y otros poemas*, *El canto errante* and *Canto a la Argentina*—all published between 1888 and 1914. *Rubén Darío: Selected Writings*, edited by Ilan Stavans, is a comprehensive anthology of his work available in English. Dario died in 1916.

Kristina Marie Darling (Books 220) is a graduate student at Washington University in St. Louis. Her work appears in the *Boston Review, Mid-American Review, New Letters* and other journals.

Ian W. Douglas (Poems 131) is a writer, photographer and designer living in Brooklyn, New York. His work has appeared in *The New Yorker* and other publications.

R. G. Evans (Poems 59) teaches and writes in southern New Jersey.

Martin Jude Farawell (Poems 76) is author of the chapbook "Genesis: A Sequence of Poems," and his work has appeared in the *The Cortland Review, Lips, Poetry East, Maryland Poetry Review, Paterson Literary Review, Paintbrush, The Southern Review, Tiferet Journal* and others, as well as a number of anthologies, including *Outsiders* from Milkweed Editions. His plays have been performed off-off-Broadway and by regional, college, community and international theaters. He directs the Geraldine R. Dodge Poetry Program.

Catalan poet **Ernest Farrés** (Poems 151) lives in Barcelona. A journalist who works on the cultural supplement of the Spanish daily, *La Vanguardia*, he has written three volumes of poetry, including *Edward Hopper*, which won the Englantina d'Or of the Jocs Florals in 2006.

Miciah Bay Gault ("City of Lonely Women" 45) is the managing editor of *Hunger Mountain* at the Vermont College of Fine Arts. Her fiction has appeared in *AGNI*. She is working on her first novel.

Argentine poet **Juan Gelman** (Poems 116) is the author of, among other books, *Violín y otras cuestiones*, *Gotán*, and *Cólera buey*; the anthology, *Unthinkable Tenderness: Selected Poems*, edited and translated by Joan Lindgren, offers a representative style of his poetry in English. He is also the author of *Dibaxu*, a volume of poetry written in Ladino, the Judeo-Spanish language. The two poems included in this issue are from that collection. Gelman taught himself the language in order to compose the book.

Alan Gilbert (Books 197) is a widely published poet and critic, and the author of *Another Future: Poetry and Art in a Postmodern Twilight*.

Deborah Hall (Books 214) is the author of *The Anatomy of Narrative: Analyzing Fiction and Creative Nonfiction*, and has published in *River Teeth: A Journal of Nonfiction Narrative*, and *International Quarterly*, among others. She is prose editor of the new online journal of Pakistan studies, *Pakistaniaat*. She teaches writing and literature at Valdosta State University in Georgia.

Huan Hsu ("Tennis Mom" 82) lives in Shanghai. This is his first published story.

J. Kates (*translator*, Poem 130) is a poet and literary translator who lives in Fitzwilliam, New Hampshire.

John Lindgren's (Poem 186) poetry and prose has appeared in *The New Yorker, The Paris Review, Chelsea, The Iowa Review, The Literary Review, Encounter, Poetry Northwest*, and is forthcoming in the *American Literary Review* and *The Southern Review*. He is working on his first book of verse, and teaches calculus and physics in Los Angeles.

A prolific man of letters in Argentina at the turn of the last century, **Leopoldo Lugones** (Poem 111) is the author of *Los crepúsculos del jardín, Lunario sentimental*, and *El payador*. He also wrote impressionistic, book-long meditations on the war against the gauchos in Argentina, and the Jesuit presence in Paraguay during colonial times. His poetry remains unavailable in English. Some of his fiction is featured in *Strange Forces*, translated into English by Gilbert Alter-Gilbert. He died in 1938.

Erica McAlpine (Poems 135) is currently finishing her PhD in English at Yale. Her poems and translations have appeared (or are forthcoming) in *Slate, TriQuarterly, The Southwest Review, Literary Imagination* and *The American Scholar*.

David McGlynn ("Wanderers in Zion" 155) is the author of the story collection *The End of the Straight and Narrow*. His recent nonfiction has appeared in *The Missouri Review, The Southwest Review, The Best American Sports Writing* and elsewhere. He teaches at Lawrence University in Wisconsin.

Matt Mendez's ("Twitching Heart" 174) writing has appeared in *BorderSenses, Alligator Juniper*, and has been nominated for a Pushcart Prize and inclusion in *Best New American Voices 2009*. His story "Airman" was winner of *Alligator Juniper*'s National Fiction Contest.

Chilean poet **Pablo Neruda** (Poem 113) received the Nobel Prize for Literature in 1970. Ilan Stavans edited the collection *The Poetry of Pablo Neruda*. Neruda translated into Spanish the work of Shakespeare, Charles Baudelaire, William Blake, Rainer Maria Rilke and James Joyce. He died in 1973.

Jennifer Louise Percy ("Training Ground" 23) is an MFA candidate at the University of Iowa's Nonfiction Writing Program. Her work has appeared or is forthcoming in *Rosebud, The Atlantic, The American Literary Review, Redivider, The Indiana Review* and *Brevity*. She is working on her first book of nonfiction.

Thomas Reiter's (Poems 62) next book of poems, *Catchment*, will be published this Fall by LSU Press. He has received poetry fellowships from the NEA and the New Jersey State Council on the Arts.

Clea Roberts (Poems 18) lives in Whitehorse, the capital city of Canada's Yukon Territory. She has published poetry in *The Malahat Review, PRISM International, The Antigonish Review, The Dalhousie Review, International Feminist Journal of Politics, Lake: A Journal of Arts and Environment*, and *Contemporary Verse 2: The Canadian Journal of Poetry and Critical Writing*, among others. She organizes the Whitehorse Poetry Festival, and her first book of poetry will be published by Freehand Books in 2010.

Paul Ruffin ("Hi-Ho, Hi-Ho, Off To The Gun Show We Go" 69) is Texas State University Regents' Professor and Distinguished Professor of English at Sam Houston State University, where he edits *The Texas Review* and directs the Texas Review Press. He is the author of two novels, three collections of short stories, six books of poetry and two collections of essays, and has edited eleven other books. He has just been named Poet Laureate of Texas.

Eric-Emmanuel Schmitt, ("The Most Beautiful Book in the World" 97) playwright, novelist and author of short stories, was awarded the French Academy's Grand Prix du Théâtre in 2001. His books include *Oscar and the Lady in Pink, The Gospel according to Pilate*, and *My life with Mozart*. The film *Odette Toulemonde*, Schmitt's debut as screenwriter and director, was released in 2007.

A.K. Scipioni (Poems 170) is a recent graduate of the Iowa Writers' Workshop. Her poems have appeared or are forthcoming in *Denver Quarterly, Diagram, Poetry Midwest, LA Miscellany*, and *1913*.

Alison Sparks (*translator*, Poem 113) is a Research Associate in the Department of Psychology at Amherst College. Her research explores the social origins of children's linguistic and cognitive development.

Ilan Stavans (*translator*, Poems 109) is Lewis-Sebring Professor in Latin American and Latino Culture at Amherst College. His books include *The Hispanic Condition, On Borrowed Words, Spanglish*, and *Love and Language*. He is the editor of *The Oxford Book of Jewish Stories, The Poetry of Pablo Neruda*, the three-volume set of *Isaac Bashevis Singer: Collected Stories*, and, to be released this October by the Library of America, *Becoming Americans: Four Hundred Years of Immigrant Writing*. His translations in this issue's mini-portfolio are part of a forthcoming anthology of twentieth-century Latin American poetry, which he edited for Farrar, Straus, and Giroux.

Nickolay Todorov ("The Dreams of Savages" 141) was born in the violent and mystical Balkans. He lives in Los Angeles, where he is a witness to and beneficiary of wild Southern California realities. His short stories have been published in *The Barcelona Review, The Pacific Review, Whiskey Island Magazine, Farmhouse Magazine, Istanbul Literary Review* and others.

Lawrence Venuti's (*translator*, Poems 151) books include *The Translator's Invisibility* and the translation of Massimo Carlotto's crime novel, *The Goodbye Kiss*. His version of Ernest Farrés's *Edward Hopper*, in which these poems appear, won the 2008 Robert Fagles Translation Prize. It will be published by Graywolf Press.

Jerald Walker ("Two Boys" 29) teaches at Bridgewater State College in Massachusetts. "Two Boys" is an excerpt from his memoir *Street Shadows: A Memoir of Race, Rebellion, and Redemption*, to be published by Random House in 2010. Other excerpts have appeared or will appear in *The Best American Essays* (2007 & 2009), *The Best African American Essays 2009* and *The Missouri Review*.

Paul-Victor Winters (Books 212) is a writer and teacher living in Southern New Jersey. Recent poems and book reviews appear or are forthcoming in *The Literary Review, The New York Quarterly,* and *Tattoo Highway*.

Marion Wyce (Books 206) has received an AWP Intro Journals Award in fiction and had her work performed in the InterAct Theatre Company's stage series Writing Aloud.

Volume 52 of *The Literary Review* consists of four numbers:
1. Fall (November 2008)   3. Spring (June 2009)
2. Winter (February 2009)   4. Summer (August 2009)
The issues of Volume 52 are paged separately, each beginning with page 1.

The index is arranged alphabetically, using the following abbreviations:

a/p	art/photography	*c*	chapbooks
e	essay	*et*	author of essay in translation
f	fiction	*ft*	author of fiction in translation
ge	guest editor	*in*	interview
l	letter	*m*	memoir
mt	memoir in translation	*nf*	non-fiction
p	poetry	*pt*	author of poetry in translation
pl	play	*plt*	play in translation
re	review essay	*t*	translator

2008-2009
Charles Angoff Awards

We are pleased to announce the twenty-fifth annual Charles Angoff Awards for outstanding contributions during a volume year.

The winners for Volume 2008-2008 (Volume 52) are:

POETRY

Aimee Nezhukumatathil (Spring 2009)
Finalist: **Clea Roberts** (Summer 2009)

FICTION

Kelly Cherry (Summer 2009)
Finalists: **Jean François Beauchemin, translated by Jessica Moore** (Fall 2008);
Miciah Bay Gault (Summer 2009); **Matt Mendez** (Summer 2009)

This cash award, named in honor of *The Literary Review*'s editor from 1957-1976, is supported by family, friends, and colleagues of the late Charles Angoff. It recognizes his initiative in helping to found *The Literary Review*, his encouragement of excellence in writing, and his own achievements as a poet, essayist, and novelist.

TLR SUBSCRIBE TODAY!

☐ **ONE YEAR US $18**
INTERNATIONAL $21

☐ **TWO YEARS US $18**
INTERNATIONAL $21

SELECT BACK ISSUES:

☐ **AFRICA CALLING** QUANTITY: ___
☐ **MODERN INDIAN POETRY** QUANTITY: ___
☐ **FALL 2008/PEN TRANSLATION** QUANTITY: ___

_____

NAME

_____

ADDRESS

_____

CITY/STATE/ZIP   COUNTRY

_____

EMAIL

☐ CHECK ENCLOSED   CHARGE MY CREDIT CARD: ☐ VISA ☐ MC ☐ AMEX

_____

CARD NUMBER   EXPIRATION DATE

_____

SIGNATURE

Send completed form to: *The Literary Review*, 285 Madison Avenue, Madison, NJ 07940 USA
Telephone: (973) 443-8564 Fax: (973) 443-8364 Email: tlr@fdu Web: www.theliteraryreview.org